Margaret Butteriss is a Senior Work Research Officer with the Work Research Unit of the Department of Employment, England. She is the author of *Job Enrichment and Employee Participation*.

Karl Albrecht, PH.D., is a management consultant, and author of *Successful Management by Objectives* and *Stress and the Manager*.

NEW
MANAGEMENT
TOOLS
Ideas and Techniques to
Help You as a Manager

MARGARET BUTTERISS
Revised by **KARL ALBRECHT**

A SPECTRUM BOOK

PRENTICE-HALL, INC., Englewood Cliffs, N.J. 07632

Library of Congress Cataloging in Publication Data

Butteriss, Margaret.
   New management tools.

   (A Spectrum Book)
   Edition of 1975 published under title: Techniques
and developments in management.
   Includes bibliographies and index.
   1. Personnel management. I. Albrecht, Karl G.
II. Title.
HF5549.B93 1979   658.3   78–11826
ISBN 0–13–615195–7
ISBN 0–13–615187–6 pbk.

Editorial/production supervision and interior design by Norma Karlin
Cover design by Jay J. Smith
Manufacturing buyers: David Hetherington and Cathie Lenard

A SPECTRUM BOOK

10 9 8 7 6 5 4 3 2 1

Printed in the United States of America

Prentice-Hall International, Inc., *London*
Prentice-Hall of Australia Pty. Limited, *Sydney*
Prentice-Hall of Canada, Ltd., *Toronto*
Prentice-Hall of India Private Limited, *New Delhi*
Prentice-Hall of Japan, Inc., *Tokyo*
Prentice-Hall of Southeast Asia Pte. Ltd., *Singapore*
Whitehall Books Limited, *Wellington, New Zealand*

Contents

Preface to the Revised Edition

A leader is best when people barely know he exists. When his work is done, his aim fulfilled, they will all say, "We did this ourselves."

Lao Tzu

That statement is at least two thousand years old. It represents an ethic for which enlightened managers have striven for a long time and which relatively few have ever approached very closely. In a sense, the history of the management profession is the history of attempts to implement this basic idea.

As we enter the last quarter of the twentieth century, we find the landscape of today's American business world vastly different from that of the beginning of the century. Our society has changed profoundly, our technology has revolutionized our lives, and our organizations are larger, more complex, and more diverse than ever before. One of the major difficulties in American business today is that our organizations and the work they do have changed more rapidly than our management theory and management practice.

We have apparently reached the limits of technocratic management methods in improving efficiency, productivity, and work output. Frederick Taylor's "scientific management," which was so well adapted to the simple industrial companies of the early century, has been stretched and extended to the limits of its applicability. We now struggle with the costly and discouraging side effects of the traditional philosophy of "production first and people second": declining productivity, widespread dissatisfaction with work, hatred and hostility as the basis of a general union–management deadlock, virtually a complete loss of pride in workmanship, and the near extinction of workers' organizational pride. Clearly, the old ways just aren't working very well any longer. Our task for the remainder of this century is therefore to preserve the technical efficiency of the management methods and techniques we've learned and to propound a new basis for humanistic management thus superseding the traditional technocratic philosophy.

This undertaking is called for because the work people do and the organizations in which they work have changed profoundly since Taylor and his contemporaries laid down the founding principles of technocratic management. Now, for example, almost nine out of ten people work in organizations of some kind, as opposed to about four out of ten in Taylor's time. Many of these organizations are quite different from any that existed then. The new phenomenon of "knowledge work," as Peter Drucker calls it, involves human creative and cognitive processes to which the Tayloristic methods are hopelessly inapplicable. We've reached the point in our technological revolution where fully 50 percent of the people in the American work force are knowledge workers—they generate, manipulate, transfer, or process information as the basic activity of their jobs. Almost 70 percent of the work force is employed in service or government jobs. Effective performance of this kind of work depends much more on the motivation and commitment of the individual worker and much less on the use of work-measurement methods and efficient design of work stations and tools.

Compounding the problem of these changes is the remarkable shift in attitudes of American workers about work, especially among younger workers who constitute the so-called "post-war baby boom." These people bring different values to their jobs, they demand more from their leaders, and they are less willing to accept authoritarian management without question. "Motivation," "job satisfaction," and "quality of work life" will surely be the bywords for the rest of this century. We must find practical ways to enable American citizens to work effectively and with a sense of commitment, at jobs that challenge their capabilities and reward them in ways they find satisfying. And we must build these patterns into the very structure of American organizations.

In the accomplishment of this goal lie the seeds for self-motivation and self-commitment by the worker. We understand by now that motivation cannot be legislated; it can only be enabled. No one, it has been said, is apathetic, except in the pursuit of someone else's objectives. We also understand now that the future basis for the economic performance of American business must be the *combination* of job satisfaction and productivity—that effective job performance tends to be an automatic consequence of job satisfaction. And we know that job satisfaction begins with the design of the job itself. We must develop a technology of job design that includes what we now know about human behavior; indeed, if Frederick Taylor were living today, he would probably be one of the strongest advocates of applying the behavioral sciences to job design.

We need to bring about two kinds of evolution in management in order to properly integrate humanistic management with technocratic management:

First, we must transform the role of the manager from that of the Commander to that of the Enabler. We must train managers thoroughly in the behavioral sciences, just as we train them thoroughly in the system sciences. That this part of the evolution is already well underway is attested to by the unprecedented demand by today's managers for training courses in behavioral science. And in my consulting work with a variety of organizations, I've met many of the "new breed" of humanistic managers.

The second, and perhaps more difficult, aspect of the evolution is in the arrangement of organizations themselves—particularly the relative distribution of power, decision-making authority, and influence over the day-to-day work of the people who make up the organization. Probably the only long-term approach to productivity and organizational effectiveness with any real promise of success is the philosophy of "participative management." This technique makes the employees of the organization more than merely workers who sell their labor for a negotiated price. Instead, they must—and most of them very much want to—become *citizens* of their organization, with a personal stake in its success and viability. As citizens of the organization, they will want and deserve to have their needs and interests considered by their leaders, and they will want a measure of influence in matters that directly affect their well-being, their morale, and their job satisfaction.

This second evolutionary process is presently underway and seems to be steadily picking up momentum. More and more American organizations are trying new and novel approaches to improving the quality of work life, in attempts to foster job satisfaction and productivity simultaneously. We are beginning to understand that the key to organizational performance—whatever kind of organization it might be—is in making the needs and interests of the employees congruent not only with the needs and interests of its managers, but also with the overall viability of the organization.

It is now becoming clear that every industrial organization has not just one "bottom line," but three: First, the traditional *economic* bottom line determines the financial survival of the organization as an entity. In the same sense, the *human* bottom line is the level of health and well-being of the people who constitute the organization. And the *social* bottom line is the sum of the effects of the organization's activities on the society and the environment around it. The practice of management in the last quarter of the twentieth century will require that the leaders of any organization successfully integrate the economic, human, and social bottom lines into a comprehensive view of the organization as a modern socio-technical system.

Carrying out this evolutionary process will require determination, a willingness to experiment and take risks, and a stock of new ideas and techniques on the part of today's managers. The manager, must supply the first two requirements. The third of these requirements constitutes the subject matter of this book. Its purpose is to provide practicing managers—at all levels and in all kinds of organizations—with an overview of promising current developments and techniques for carrying out the orderly and constructive evolution of management practice.

Originally written in England, the book reflected British and European applications of these various techniques; Margaret Butteriss has done an excellent job of compiling and explaining a variety of important topics. My task in revising the volume has been to retain the essence of her excellent analysis, while shifting the emphasis and the case examples to the American setting. I place myself at the reader's mercy to decide how well I've handled my task. It's only fair to accord Ms. Butteriss the credit for the quality of the concepts and to accept for myself the responsibility for any obscurity in the presentation. However, at the risk of seeming immodest, I do feel we've achieved an effective partnership across the Atlantic, and I hope you'll find the results interesting and worth reading.

I have modified the original edition in several ways. I've added a number of techniques and developments that seem distinctly American and that at present don't seem to have taken hold in England or on the Continent. I've also deleted a few topics from the original that are rather commonplace in American management practice, although they are relatively new in European settings: These include performance appraisals, job evaluation, and staff status for manual workers. Topics I've added include career development, problem counseling, stress-reduction training, assertive communication training, transactional analysis, Scanlon Plans, assessment centers, equal employment opportunity, and behavior modification. Several of the other original topics that seemed interesting but somewhat controversial and as yet unproven I chose to include anyway, in a section set aside for very new and experimental techniques.

If you, the reader, use this book as we hope you will, you'll read it to get a comprehensive overview of current methods and trends in the management field. You will then think them over, analyze and discuss them with your colleagues, experiment with those that seem worthwhile to you, study the results, modify them, or invent others to suit your needs and your views. Above all, trade the results with your colleagues.

For in the end, you, the practicing manager, are the one who really establishes management theory and management method. You convert speculation to practice, as well as sort out the winning ideas from those that "also ran." I know of no more significant challenge facing us as managers today than the challenge of humanizing our business organizations and of mobilizing human effort in ways that are not only economically viable but also rewarding and supportive for the citizens of our organizations.

Press on. And good luck!

KARL ALBRECHT, Ph.D.
San Diego

Introduction

The Content

Directed primarily to people who are new to the personnel and management fields, this book describes current and important developments that influence the organization and affect personnel management, directly or indirectly. Its purpose is not to describe older established techniques and developments, such as recruitment and selection, wage and salary administration, and the like, since these are already well documented. The developments and techniques chosen, and consequently the book, can be divided into three sections:

Section One essentially states that the individual should be given the opportunity to achieve greater satisfaction from his/her work and greater control over the work environment. It is hoped that the satisfaction of individual needs will help the achievement of corporate objectives. Included in this category are:

Job rotation

Job enrichment

Job enlargement

Autonomous work groups

Participative management

Flexible working hours

Career development

Problem counseling

Stress-reduction training

Assertive communication training

Transactional analysis

Section Two includes approaches and trends that are aimed at achieving organizational needs and that have arisen from the need for efficient organization where human resources are utilized effectively. Labor can no longer be regarded as a cheap resource and must therefore be used in the best possible way. This category contains largely methods for the control of labor usage in achieving organizational objectives.

Human resources planning

Scanlon Plan

Assessment centers

Management by objectives

Organization development

Equal employment opportunity

Behavior modification

Section Three includes techniques and developments so new or controversial that no firm basis exists for evaluating their effectiveness. Most of them have arisen in Europe, and their place in American management methodology is questionable. They do, however, warrant careful study in terms of their potential for increasing organizational effectiveness. This section includes:

Human resource accounting

Employee directors

Supervisory boards

Common ownership

The Method

Wherever feasible, the approach to the study of these topics will take the following format:

A brief description of the development

How and why it originated

The various ways it can be implemented

Examples

Advantages

Disadvantages/Problems

Further reading

Section One

INDIVIDUAL NEEDS

This section is concerned with techniques and developments connected with the concept that individuals should be given the opportunity to satisfy their needs at work, as well as greater control over their work environment.

1

Job Rotation

Job rotation is the movement of workers among various tasks that are either similar or dissimilar. Movement usually takes place at regular intervals ranging from a few hours to several weeks.

Rotation has been introduced at operator level as a means of introducing variety into a job and of thus alleviating boredom. When it is introduced at management level, where rotation may take place every six months or so, it can be seen as a phase in management development. At this level it is often aimed at developing an individual, at helping him or her appreciate the many functions within an organization, and ultimately at preparing that person for a top position. It also provides for an assessment of future potential. In this context rotation may be seen as planning for future manpower requirements.

In this section attention is focused largely on operator rotation.

Examples

Fruit Canning Factory

This example, one in which I was directly involved, was an attempt to make time pass more quickly!

The factory, organized on the traditional conveyor belt system, was set up to can fruit. The factory staff consisted largely of middle aged women, with a small number of men doing the heavier jobs. But because of the large quantities of strawberries that had to be canned during the summer months, a number of students were employed on a temporary basis. All the work was unskilled.

The students (including me) were generally employed on the conveyor belt as follows:

1. placing cans from a large cardboard box onto the conveyor belt,

2. placing differing sizes and grades of strawberries in the cans, and

3. weighing the cans before they were sealed and placed in the ovens.

Because the work was so repetitive and boring, the eight-hour day passed very slowly; the student group therefore decided to rotate their three jobs. This was to be an informal system, and rotation would take place every twenty minutes. Once we had introduced this system, time passed much more quickly and there was greater opportunity for interaction.

But the foreman in charge was far from happy with this system and finally prevented us from rotating jobs. None of us left as a result, because we had to tolerate the job for only a few weeks and the pay was too good. But we were a considerably more disgruntled work force. Interestingly enough, the older women did not even consider rotation as they were quite happy to spend all day in their own little groups, talking to one another.

Renault

At the Le Mans factory of Renault, where front and back axles for the whole range of Renault cars are assembled, traditionally each worker does one of the sixty operations while the line of partly made axles moves in front of him.

Management realized that a change was required in the system. There were a large number of wildcat strikes, and the immigrant workers who make up most of the labor force have become dissatisfied with working conditions, which are tedious, boring, and often dangerous.

One attempt at change has been the introduction of job rotation. Each man changes his job every hour so that his routine is broken and he does not get physical and mental cramps.

Advantages

1. Operators can acquire skill in various activities, which can lead to better promotion prospects.

2. Job rotation can increase job interest due to changes in environment, skill requirement, and job content.

3. It is advantageous from management's point of view because it increases the operator's skill and flexibility.

Disadvantages/Problems

1. Loss of routine, which can lead to a decrease in output.

2. More time may be lost due to movement from job to job.

3. Sometimes there may be a loss of status for the operator, if jobs vary in status or skill level.

4. Inefficiency may result from job moves, initially, due to a lack of familiarity in the job.

2

Job Enrichment

Job enrichment is the redesign of a job to include tasks and activities that promote the psychological involvement of the worker in the job itself. It includes rearranging tasks and processes, adding new tasks, increasing feedback on results and performance, increasing task variety, and increasing the level of contact with other workers.

The need for job enrichment was recognized when behavioral scientists like Douglas McGregor and Frederick Herzberg pointed out that most individuals were more motivated when they were given opportunities to exercise discretion and given more responsibility. McGregor's Theory Y sees man as an essentially creative being who will seek responsibility, exercise discretion and self-control, and see achievement as its own reward. According to Herzberg's motivation/hygiene theory, an individual is motivated when he or she is given opportunities for self-advancement, self-development, achievement, recognition, and advancement arising from an interesting and demanding job.

Although American writers have had more to say about job enrichment than European experts, European and Scandinavian firms probably have actually experimented more with it.

Ways of Enriching Jobs

1. Giving a worker a whole job with an identifiable end product and allowing the individual more freedom to set targets.

2. Redesigning work so that a whole job on an identifiable unit of work is carried out, and so that a person or team is given authority and discretion for that unit of work.

3. Reducing or changing the level of supervision. Supervision becomes supportive, concentrating on advising work groups on how to achieve their targets, rather than exercising close control. Controls are therefore removed, but the individual is still accountable for his or her tasks.

4. Some methods of job enrichment have led to discretion over work pace. For instance, in the Saab car as-

sembly plant a girl assembler can complete one car engine alone in thirty minutes, or three girls can work together and complete an engine in 10 minutes, thus allowing choice over work method and pace.

5. Introducing more difficult and exacting jobs and giving more immediate feedback of results.

Reasons for Job Enrichment

1. High wages have led to the need for better use of people; some form of job restructuring can often achieve this result.

2. Today's worker is often better educated than his or her older counterpart, and consequently expects more from the job. If dissatisfied at work, an individual can express this attitude by poor workmanship, absenteeism, and high labor turnover. For these reasons Saab and Volvo in Sweden redesigned their assembly line, in an attempt to prevent high absenteeism and labor turnover figures. It is felt, although not yet proved, that better motivated people may result from such schemes.

3. Changes in the production line systems of the British car industry, where labor turnover is low, have largely been undertaken for technical reasons such as cutting production costs, improving production, increasing flexibility and the quality of the product. Job enrichment in this case has largely been concentrated on the individual rather than on the work team. For instance,

Ford made changes in its gearbox assembly. Instead of parts moving along a conveyor belt for an individual to pick up and assemble, the worker was able to move round a hanging carrier, and assemble a number of different parts. However, nothing was left to chance: The worker had to assemble the parts in a set order and at a set pace, and thus there was no increase in discretion.

4. In Holland and Scandinavia, job enrichment has been introduced in order to give workers more discretion and has generally centered on semi-autonomous work groups, who do their own checking and inspection.

Examples

Cutler–Hammer

In Cutler–Hammer's Milwaukee assembly plant, management employed job enrichment in an effort to improve the effectiveness of an assembly line. Workers stood at a row of segregated work stations along a straight conveyor, assembling electrical equipment in a sequence of operations. The design of the line was faulty to begin with, since even though the execution times for the various tasks were significantly different, the conveyor moved at a constant speed. In addition, the work area was uncomfortable, poorly lighted, chilly, and subject to hazard from passing vehicles. The workers in the target group exhibited one of the poorest safety records in the plant, and their rates of absenteeism and turnover were the highest.

In redesigning the process, management removed the conveyor and rearranged the work flow into a U-shaped pattern. They also removed the partitions, enabling the workers to operate together in a smaller area. Each person executed his or her part of the assembly operation, passing the part to an intake tray beside the next person down the line. Whenever one work station began to lag behind the others, someone from a downstream station moved to that station to help reduce the backlog. In this way, workers moved about among the various assembly points and had much more opportunity for a variety of experiences and interpersonal contact. Despite the removal of the conveyor, the average assembly rate increased by 7 percent.

A group incentive plan instituted along with the work redesign also enabled the workers to earn more money. Other aspects of the redesigned work situation led to greater team spirit, higher morale, and greater overall levels of satisfaction with the job.

Richard Baxendale and Sons, Ltd., England

This company manufactures heating units and has risen from one hundred to eight hundred employees in ten years. This rapid growth of the company caused concern at bringing the management style up to date; and so "works councils," consisting of shop stewards and office representatives, together with job restructuring have been introduced. This has been coupled with the replacement of the piecework system by a job evaluation system.

Four experiments in job enrichment have been tried in order to try to introduce more job satisfaction. In the *first* experiment four people were involved in a flow line producing burners. The group was simply told that they were expected to keep their output at the same level but that they could organize the work as they liked. This plan was immediately successful and produced no problems.

The *second* experiment concerned eight women who worked in sequence on an assembly line producing transformer boxes for burners. Management felt that one woman could easily assemble a whole box, and so a person who had had no prior experience on the job was recruited and taught to assemble the whole box. Unfortunately, however, this girl was completely isolated from her work colleagues and left after only one month.

The *third* experiment involved nine skilled sheet metal workers, who were renowned for their ability to beat the piecework system. They used to work on a production line system in sheet metal structures, but now a worker was allowed to complete a whole unit himself. Absenteeism dropped and the quality of the work improved, but the men suspected that this was a plot to remove piecework and so returned to the old system. As soon as piecework was abandoned in the company as a whole, they opted to return to the restructured jobs.

The *fourth* experiment involved sixty men assembling quite complex control units for boilers. At the end of each line the controls were tested. To make this system more interesting and to achieve more flexibility in the work force, it was decided that the men should be given complete freedom of choice as to how they would like to assemble the controls. If he chose to do so, a man could work on his own or with any number of colleagues. Most people opted to work in groups of three, and each group was responsible for testing its own set and correcting any faults.

As a result of this experiment the company has encouraged the men to increase their skills and job responsibility; it has not brought about any increase in costs. There is also a payoff in terms of greater flexibility and less absenteeism.

Advantages

A study of the case histories of organizations that have introduced this system indicates that several advantages accrue:

1. It leads to a multi-skilled work force who can do a number of jobs, so there is no real problem if key people are absent.

2. An individual can often work at his or her own pace; this self-pacing can reduce a number of physical and emotional problems.

3. Because individuals and work teams are semi-autonomous and do their own checking and inspection, there is a reduction in the number of supervisors required.

4. Often this technique leads to a reduction in absenteeism and turnover, although further research is required to see how far job enrichment is really responsible for these changes. Further, an increase in productivity and an improvement in the quality of work usually occur.

Although there are advantages to job enrichment, this technique does engender a number of problems and these must be thoroughly considered before such a scheme is implemented.

Disadvantages/Problems

1. This system highlights the need for good selection and training so that suitable people, who like increased responsibility, are engaged and then given thorough training.

2. The costs of retooling or redesigning the plant may be so high, along with the need for extra space, that it may completely offset savings caused by lower labor turnover and absenteeism.

3. The climate and culture must be right. All levels of management, as well as lower-level workers, must be committed to change or the system will not work. An effective system of communication is essential.

4. Job enrichment is not easy to introduce or execute in operations that do not result in a tangible end product as, say, in the case of research; in such a case, who contributed most to the scheme is difficult to say.

5. Job enrichment may take a while to introduce as people take time to adjust to changes and to work under a new work method requiring cohesive work teams.

6. Agreement with unions is essential in such matters as manning ratios, redeployment, and training.

7. Job enrichment must not be considered as a substitute for an appropriate pay scheme. If the pay system is not considered fair, no amount of job enrichment will bring adequate job satisfaction. Payment systems must be right before attempting to introduce any change in the way people do jobs.

Further Reading

BUTTERISS, MARGARET, *Job Enrichment and Employee Participation.* London: Institute for Personnel Management, 1971.

HERZBERG, FREDERICK, *Work and the Nature of Man.* New York: John Wiley & Sons, Inc., 1959.

MCGREGOR, DOUGLAS, *The Human Side of Enterprise.* New York: McGraw-Hill Book Company, 1961.

3

Job Enlargement

Job enlargement describes changes that increase the variety or scope of tasks to be carried out by the individual. Job enlargement can be seen as one of a variety of job-enrichment techniques.

Interest in job enlargement has developed largely as a reaction to the increasing specialization and simplification of work in modern industry. This technique is used to alleviate problems of fatigue, frustration, low morale, and feelings of apathy created by specialization. Modern theorists argue that monotony, boredom, absenteeism, lateness, and job changes are also side effects of work simplification. An enlargement program attempts to reverse job specialization by giving employees more scope with varied tasks for the use of more knowledge and a greater variety of skills. Presumably, increased variation, longer work cycles, and the worker's knowledge that he or she has produced a whole unit should increase the operator's output and lead to greater job satisfaction.

Two principal avenues for job enlargement are "vertical job loading" and "horizontal job loading." The term *loading* refers to the extent to which certain kinds of tasks and requirements are included in the structure of the job. Enlarging a job by increased *vertical* loading means adding tasks or responsibilities that call for greater responsibility, authority, discretion, or autonomy. By implication, some functions are transferred from the supervisor to the employee. *Horizontal* job loading refers to adding tasks or functions that are on the same level of responsibility and authority as those presently included in the job.

Vertical enlargement of a cashier's job, for example, might include adding the responsibility of totaling up the register, separating currency, balancing against receipts, and preparing a cash summary. Horizontal enlargement of the same job might include adding such tasks as giving information to customers, handling returned or exchanged merchandise, and training or assisting other employees.

Examples

IBM, Endicott, New York

One of the first companies to practice job enlargement was IBM at its plant in Endicott, New York, where new management techniques and technological changes were introduced between 1940 and 1949. Job content was substantially enlarged for workers and foremen and consequently reduced for middle management. At the same time the technology changed to continuous assembly work. The levels of supervision were reduced, and, with the elimination of department heads, foremen were closer to top management. These changes led to simpler and quicker communication, and operators were able to integrate more satisfactorily with their fellow workers at all levels. Greater cooperation evolved, which meant fewer crises, and those crises that did occur were solved more quickly. The enlargement of the job was seen as leading to a more challenging, demanding, and satisfying work environment.

Ford Motor Company

Ford applied job enlargement techniques to the assembly of shock absorbers in its Escort assembly plant in Germany. About one hundred of the seven thousand workers had their jobs redesigned. Instead of each worker adding only one or two small parts to each of the shock absorbers moving along on the assembly conveyor, now each person assembles a complete shock absorber. Accompanying a shock absorber unit from station to station along the assembly line, the worker has a chance to move about rather than stand rooted to one location. Workers operate in small groups, controlling their own pace and break schedules. Though they work to the same production quota previously required, they decide for themselves how to meet it. Each group elects a leader, and holds bi-weekly meetings to work out production problems. Ford managers are quite satisfied with productivity, and they report

very high levels of morale among the experimental workers.

Renault

At the Renault axle factory in Le Mans, France, a
system has been introduced that allows workers to follow
the moving line, instead of the line moving past them.
About twenty men move between a slowly moving axle in
front of them and slowly moving parts suspended in the
air behind them. Instead of bolting on just one component
they do twenty-two operations in about five minutes,
stamp the final product with their names, and lift it on to
an overhead transporter.

This system has been tried on three lines since 1972
and has involved eighty-eight people. The major differ-
ence between the enlarged job system and the traditional
method is that each operator can work at his or her own
rhythm and speed. The worker who finishes work early
can take lunch early or have a longer rest period. The
workers claim that they have to think harder but that the
system makes them feel more like their own bosses.

The advantages to the company are shown in a 30
percent reduction of accidents, because of job enlargement and the introduction of new machines. Furthermore
work output is now higher and products are of better quality. One spin-off benefit has been the elimination of the
job of the "hooker," the worker who lifted axles and put
them on the overhead conveyor. This was considered to be
the most boring and least skilled job.

Problems arose in the initial setting up because of
everyone's lack of experience in this field, but start-up

difficulties were gradually overcome by the introduction of more training.

Philips Telecommunication of Australia, Ltd.

This subsidiary of Philips Industry produced mobile radio equipment using an assembly line process. Women worked on assembly lines producing either individual small sub-assemblies or combining sub-assemblies into finished radios. Between one and five stages were involved, and no job cycle was greater than twenty minutes.

This system proved inefficient, largely because predicting customer demand for number and type was difficult. Thus stocking a large number of finished products was necessary, which was costly. Further, poor workmanship was evident. The women complained that frequent job changes meant they did not spend enough time on one job to develop the required speed; thus their production bonus was lower.

In 1966 it was decided to introduce job enlargement. Under the new scheme the *total* assembly of any one type of mobile radio from individual components was done by each operator, and each was responsible for her own inspection. Instruction sheets were given to the operators, and women were trained individually by the foreman.

This system enabled the company to reduce its investments in stocks. As each complete radio was assembled from individual components by one person, it was no longer necessary to retain stocks of sub-assemblies. Further, the longer job cycle made it easier to switch over from the production of one kind of mobile radio to another. These two factors allowed the value of inventories to be reduced dramatically.

The new method also led to a considerable improvement in quality. Other spin-offs have been better short-term commercial planning and a reduced use of indirect staff (for example, inspectors). The challenge of the enlarged job is seen as a great source of satisfaction by the workers.

Advantages

1. It appears to lead to reduced operator fatigue and a relief from the boredom of highly specialized and repetitive work.

2. It allows the operator to exercise more control over individual working speed and to use more skills.

Disadvantages/Problems

1. An increase in the personal satisfaction of employees may not outweigh the fact that this system can sometimes be technically less efficient than the more specialized arrangement.

2. There may be limited scope for job enlargement in some situations because of production systems.

3. Overcoming resistance to change is one problem that

can arise, particularly among senior workers who are thoroughly conditioned to the assembly line system.

4. Consideration must be given to increased training time.

Further Reading

PAULING, T., "Job Enlargement—on Experience at Philips Telecommunications of Australia, Ltd.," *Personnel Practice Bulletin* (September 1968).

4

Autonomous Work Groups

Autonomous work groups are result-oriented groups of workers, often largely independent of external controls or influences for substantial periods. They are normally responsible for the assembly of a complete unit or sub-unit, for the manning of certain equipment, or for a complete area of work. Such groups are often also responsible for quality inspection, organizing and planning their workload, for problem-solving, and for machinery maintenance. The members of these groups are usually trained to perform all or most of the tasks carried out within the group; thus they are all multi-skilled and have considerable responsibility.

Such groups have been introduced for a number of reasons. They may be a natural progression from the enrichment of the individual's job. More likely they are introduced because individuals' jobs cannot be enlarged or enriched without reorganizing the work of the whole department or process. In such cases job redesign may have led to the assembly line being abandoned in favor of autonomous work groups working on complete modules.

The majority of firms that have changed to this system have done so either to reduce costs or to increase productivity. Many were suffering from high labor turnover and absenteeism, which of course did not help costs or productivity.

Examples

Rushton Mining Company

One of the most widely reported and studied examples of autonomous work groups is in the Rushton Mining Company, in Pennsylvania. In 1973, Rushton executives collaborated with consultants from Carnegie Mellon University to design a new approach to the various tasks involved in the subsurface mining of coal. Workers were formed into operating teams, with the responsibility for deciding among themselves how they would schedule their work activities, how individuals would be assigned to the various jobs, and how they would meet production goals. The role of foreman was changed from the traditional power-oriented, authoritarian parent figure to that of a coach, problem-solver, and supporting expert. Foremen were no longer permitted to operate by giving isolated direct instructions to the miners on a piecemeal basis. Instead, they became participants in the group processes of deciding how the work was to be done. In addition, they took on extra duties in the areas of training and safety.

In addition to much improved morale, team spirit, and relationships between foremen and miners, Rushton management reports dramatically reduced accident rates, closer adherence to safety techniques and procedures, and reduced costs for parts and supplies.

Philips Industries

One of the first European companies to introduce autonomous work groups was Philips Industries at its television plant in Eindhoven in the Netherlands, with the aim of promoting stronger motivation.

A group of seven people was set up to assemble a complete television receiver. Each member of the group deals with a complete sub-unit of the set, but each is also free to decide how to complete that part. Group members help each other with production problems and take over from those who are absent. They are all in direct contact with the stores, the quality department, and the repair and maintenance group. They may ask the department manager for help and advice as and when required.

Data are recorded by the group on production and quality, and discussions between the group and management take place when discussing this data is necessary.

The advantages of the system are:

1. The group is more flexible and less sensitive to interruption.

2. Cooperation and satisfaction are high.

3. Operators can control their own pace.

4. Faults are remedied immediately.

On the basis of this experience and other experiments, Philips feels that success with an autonomous work group requires certain characteristics:

1. The number of the group should be between four and ten.

2. Coaches should be available to each group for advice.

3. Management should only give a rough layout and distribution of tasks, but the group should plan the precise details itself.

4. Group members should be equal in production capabilities.

5. It is helpful if members of the work group do not have more than ten years age gap between them.

6. Training is required on how to work autonomously.

Advantages

1. Employees appear to enjoy job satisfaction and higher morale.

2. Absenteeism and labor turnover tend to decrease.

3. Often production flexibility increases.

4. Employees often become more committed to standards of workmanship and production performance.
5. Supervision and communication are improved.

Disadvantages/Problems

1. More machinery or other capital equipment may be needed.
2. This approach may be applied mostly to industries that have traditionally used production line methods, and it therefore may not be applicable to the newer, high-technology industries.
3. Some supervisors may have difficulty dealing with newly autonomous workers, possibly feeling less "needed" and less in control.

Further Reading

National Center for Productivity and Quality of Working Life, *Alternatives in the World of Work.* Washington, D.C., winter 1976.

5

Participative Management

Participative management changes the conventional relationships between managers and employees in various ways to increase the amount of influence employees have in the overall direction of the organization. This concept has been rather slow to develop in the United States. Some programs and approaches have involved substantial employee influence, while others have simply amounted to traditional forms of the union–management struggle done up in different clothing. Some management groups have even chosen to delude themselves about participative management by applying the term to their collective bargaining activities—which in reality are required by labor law. True participative management, however, involves a voluntary and reciprocal redefinition of the traditional worker–manager–organization relationship, in specific ways that make employee inputs a natural part of the process of conducting the organization's business.

In some cases, *labor–management committees* have succeeded in carrying out effective participative programs. Though a large number of unionized companies in America have labor–management committees, perhaps only a small fraction of them can be said to have brought about major changes in organizational philosophy. Thus far, the labor–management committee has principally had the effect of generally reducing tension and improving understanding between company representatives and union leaders. This is, of course, a worthwhile goal in itself, but it falls far short of constituting participative management. Even so, such efforts can lead to enough improvements in the overall social climate and in the relationship between top managers and union leaders that participative management programs can eventually be instituted.

Some European companies have developed participative management approaches that would seem quite radical in the United States, yet these programs have shown very positive results. Some of these experiments have included the placing of employee representatives on company boards of directors, the forming of "supervisory boards" composed of employees and even community representatives who oversee the operation of the conventional board of directors, and the employee ownership of an entire company by internal distribution of shares. Chapters 20, 21, and 22 describe these experimental techniques in greater depth.

The present discussion focuses on participative management approaches based on the more familiar forms of labor–management interaction such as are likely in America. Such programs in this country usually involve the formation of employee groups, often within nonunion organizations. These groups collect the ideas, opinions, values, and desires of the employees, and then they make this information available to top management for incorporation in the planning and direction of the the organization. The purpose of the employee group in this case is not to form a power bloc to counteract the efforts of management, but to focus the inputs of all employees by means of a common forum.

Examples

Harman International Industries

The Automotive Division of Harman International Industries, located in Bolivar, Tennessee, has been one of the noteworthy examples of unprecedented cooperation and constructive interaction between workers and managers. Beginning in 1973, Harman management began to collaborate closely with the leaders of the local union of the United Auto Workers. The result was a program aimed at simultaneously improving the quality of working life within the plant and increasing productivity on the company's principal product, automobile mirrors.

The improved spirit of cooperation between union leaders and managers, the increased contribution of ideas by rank-and-file employees, and the positive feedback for those ideas led to a variety of significant improvements in company operations. According to Board Chairman Dr. Sidney Harman, the significant achievements of the program included:

1. an increase in individual productivity from $132 to $165 per day,

2. a significant reduction in absences and turnover,

3. the workers' acceptance of responsibility for quality assurance in their own work,

4. the maintenance of profit levels while reducing product prices to meet increasing competition,

5. a cost-saving program, with sharing of benefits from cost reduction,

6. union participation in preparing bids for major contracts, and

7. the development of a company school where employees increase work-related skills and pursue non-work-related interests.

James B. Lansing Sound, Inc.

A subsidiary of Harman International, James B. Lansing Sound, Inc., located in Northridge, California, is another example of a similar cooperative effort. JBL, a non-union company, works with a volunteer employee committee that meets regularly to study current problems and opportunities for improving the quality of working life within the organization, as well as for improving product quality and increasing productivity. Middle managers serve as advisors to the committee, but play no direct part in its control. JBL's top management has found the employee group to be highly responsible and to advocate practical, realistic changes of benefit to the company and employees both. They report very high levels of morale and employee commitment, resulting from the feeling of having a significant part to play in steering the course of the company.

TVA

The Tennessee Valley Authority is another organization committed to participative management. The original structure and management policies of the TVA emphasized labor–management cooperation from its inception. The three-member Board of Directors established a written policy on "systematic employee–management cooperation" in 1935, which read:

> As a further development of this policy the Board of Directors looks forward to the establishment of joint conferences between the duly authorized representatives of the supervised employees and the supervisory and management staff for the purpose of systematic employee–management cooperation. The Board recognizes that responsible organizations and associations of employees are helpful to such cooperation.

Even before the various employees working for the TVA had become fully organized, TVA management began to work with them and to solicit cooperation and

suggestions for effective operation and employee job satisfaction.

Over the years, each of the major operating sites and
facilities throughout the valley developed labor–
management committees of roughly similar form. A typical committee has two co-chairmen representing labor and
management, a secretary, and an equal number of union
and management representatives. One of the most important purposes of the committee is to foster constructive
suggestions from managers and workers alike concerning
the improvement of operations. Although TVA pays no
cash awards for the suggestions, the average rate reported
for 1973 was forty-eight suggestions per one hundred
employees. Workers frequently comment on their feelings
of involvement and sense of efficacy in helping to run the
operation efficiently.

These committee actions also provide a valuable sec-
ondary benefit. New ideas that might eventually form the
basis of contract negotiations can be tried out on a small
scale. If they show promise for the organization and the
employees both, they can easily move to the stages of consideration and adoption during the collective bargaining
process. If not, they can be discarded or modified with
little impact on operational effectiveness and labor–
management relations.

Advantages

Programs that give employees an adequate voice in matters concerning their welfare tend to improve the overall
organizational climate, often dramatically. The resulting

feelings of personal significance, involvement, and sense of efficacy gained from having a say in the overall operation can lead them to develop not only a sense of commitment to the organization, but also a desire to see it succeed. Although feelings of pride in one's organization seem relatively rare in American business, participative management programs can indeed foster those feelings. These positive attitudes tend to prevent or reverse the frequently negative effects of formal union–management struggles, and in fact they may even facilitate the process of collective bargaining.

Specific advantages claimed include:

1. improved morale,

2. more efficient communications up and down the organization,

3. earlier detection and action on operational problems,

4. the simultaneous improvement in worker satisfaction and productivity,

5. increased trust between employees and managers,

6. reduced absenteeism and turnover,

7. a greater willingness on the part of management to institute changes beneficial to workers,

8. greater employee support of management plans and actions,

9. improvement in union–management relations in unionized organizations, and

10. improvement in the competitive position of a company through greater operating efficiency.

Disadvantages/Problems

Disadvantages stem mostly from errors in implementation, such as:

1. feelings of apprehension on the part of managers about the loss of control,

2. an initial period of disorientation among employees, especially if the changes are abrupt,

3. the opposition of some labor leaders to such programs if they suspect their influence may decline,

4. the preference of some labor leaders for a rigid adversary relationship with top management, as a means to avoid becoming accountable for operational effectiveness,

5. scuttling by management's insincerity or lack of commitment, making the program a sham by using it to weaken union influence or by merely paying it lip service, or

6. a lack of managers with relatively well-developed human relations skills and of involved key employees in the program.

Further Reading

National Center for Productivity and Quality of Working Life, *Alternatives in the World of Work*. Washington, D.C., winter 1976.

National Center for Productivity and Quality of Working Life, *Labor–Management Productivity Committees in American Industry.* Washington, D.C., May 1975.

National Center for Productivity and Quality of Working Life, *Recent Initiatives in Labor–Management Cooperation.* Washington, D.C., February 1976.

6

Flexible Working Hours (Flextime)

Flexible working hours, or *flextime,* is a system whereby individuals can come and go to work as they please, so long as they work a specified number of hours each accounting period. Generally this accounting period is four weeks, but there are many variations.

Until recently most companies used the system of fixed working hours, with fixed starting and finishing times each day. Each employee must be at work at the appointed time, and often deductions are made from the pay of workers who are consistently late.

Flexible working hours, as its name implies, allows an individual to be flexible about the time he or she starts and finishes work. Under this system a plant or other work facility is open between, say, 8:00 A.M. and 7:00 P.M. Staff may arrive any time between 8:00 and 10:00 A.M. and leave any time between 4:00 and 7:00 P.M. Everyone must be at work between 10:00 A.M. and 4:00 P.M. and this period is referred to as *core-time*. Employees work a certain number of hours over a set period, which may be a week or a month. A worker who has worked more hours than necessary can take the excess as time off during the next period; one who has not worked sufficient hours can make up the debit during that time too.

Variations

A number of variations will be considered in order of flexibility, starting with the least flexible.

Flexibility Within a Work Day

The simplest and most basic type of flextime, this version gives the employee a minimum amount of freedom to decide on working hours according to personal preference. The typical characteristics of such a system are:

Starting band   — 8:00 A.M.–9:30 A.M.
Core time   — 9:30 A.M.–4:30 P.M.
Finishing band   — 4:30 P.M.– 7:00 P.M.

A person will have to work, say, eight hours each day, and there is no carry-over of debit or credit to the next day.

This system can determine when a person arrives at work and finishes, but, if the lunch break is fixed, the starting time automatically determines the finishing time. Greater flexibility can be introduced if there is a flexible lunch break of, say, 12:00 until 2:00 P.M. Employees are then allowed to decide the duration of their lunch break, provided they have a minimum of, say, half an hour. With a fixed lunch break, the day looks like this:

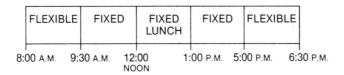

With a flexible lunch break it looks like this:

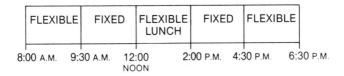

Flexibility Within the Work Week

The main advantage to the employee in this system is that the finishing time is no longer directly controlled by the starting time. The obligation is to work the required number of hours per week, but the worker can vary the daily schedule more to suit his or her own convenience.

Flexibility Within the Work Month

Under such a system the employee must work a contracted number of hours per month, so he or she can vary not only the daily schedule but the weekly schedule too.

Flexibility Within the Work Month
with Carry-Forward

Under this system the employee is not even required to work a fixed number of hours per month. He or she is allowed to be in credit or debit within certain specified limits. These limits vary from company to company usually within seven to eighteen hours. The ability to carry forward either a debit or a credit into the next month gives the employee the ability to vary a work schedule over longer periods.

Flexibility Within the Work Month
with Carry-Forward Plus Core-Time Off

This is the most flexible system that has been implemented. Not only can an employee carry forward credit or debit hours from one month to the next, but he or she may use credit hours to take a half-day or a whole day off, depending on the policy of the organization. The number of hours worked can be recorded on manual time sheets or by time clocks.

Extensions of the Flextime Concept

A variety of other approaches to the flexible use of human resources are becoming increasingly popular, especially with large organizations. Alternative work patterns include *permanent part-time* arrangements, wherein employees who can only be available to work a certain portion of the day—such as mothers with child-care responsibilities—can have the status and benefits of regular employees, but scaled down in proportion to the amount of time they work. Properly assigned, these employees can be highly productive, and there are usually few negative side effects to the organization. Indeed, part-timers can even be a valuable source of fill-in labor, to help level out periods of imbalance in the overall workload. This scheme also enables organizations to employ handicapped people more effectively, who may need time off for medical treatment, rehabilitation, or occasional rest and recuperation.

Job sharing is a similar approach, in which two part-time workers work at more or less the same job, each contributing on his or her own schedule. Of course, this technique can be applied only to carefully selected jobs, and the workers must coordinate carefully through the supervisor.

Examples

Messerschmidt Boelkow Blohm GmBH

One of the first organizations to experiment with flextime was Messerschmidt Boelkow Blohm GmBH, whose headquarters were located on the outskirts of Munich. In 1967, the personnel manager, Herr Hilbert, was concerned about the considerable amount of unrest caused by overcrowded public transportation conditions in the vicinity of the factory and the queuing that resulted from the compulsory clocking-in arrangements. The personnel manager experimented with a staggered working day and "variable working hours" that gave the employees some freedom to choose when they attended work. He ultimately came up with the idea of flexible working time, which involved a core-time when everyone has to be present and flexible times when employees have variable starting and finishing times.

Social Security Administration

One of the largest applications of flextime was at the Baltimore facility of the Social Security Administration. About half of the nine thousand employees were involved in the experiment, which began in 1974. Eighty percent of the employees were women, who made extensive use of sick leave and short-term hourly leave. Most of them also depended heavily on local transportation to travel to and from work.

Managers at the facility instituted the flextime system in hopes of alleviating several problems: the exhausting of sick leave by most employees, amounting to thirteen working days per year, periods of nonproductivity possibly due to inefficient utilization of the work force, extensive excused absences, and extensive use of unpaid leave. Many of these problems seemed connected to the general low level of morale and widespread feelings of boredom and detachment from the routine clerical work. Managers hoped that flextime would improve morale, facilitate the use of leave, help with child-care and transportation problems, and improve productive time on the job.

The facility managers conducted a thorough employee information program before making any changes. They explained the reasoning behind the proposed changes and how the new system would work. Offices would remain open between 6:30 A.M. and 6:00 P.M. The work day remained at eight hours, with supervisory coverage maintained throughout the day.

After a test period, both employees and managers concluded that the flextime system was highly effective, and Administration officials have decided to extend it to a larger number of employees. Results included an immediate increase in productivity, which remained at the higher level. "Lateness" to work became almost nonexistent, since employees accepted responsibility for a full eight-hour working day. Leave problems were eased, and many workers reported greater convenience in child-care arrangements and career development activities.

The union favored the system and concurred with supervisors at various levels in wanting it extended to cover more workers.

Advantages

A general view of the organizations that have introduced flextime indicates that a number of advantages and disadvantages can occur, although these may not be present at any one time in any one organization. For convenience's sake, the advantages and disadvantages are divided into separate categories for management and employees.

Management Advantages

1. Most managers who have introduced flextime seem to believe that the employees have developed a more responsible attitude towards their work. Jobs in hand

tend to be finished, and team spirit is encouraged where individuals have to consult each other before making a group decision about starting and finishing times. Flextime has eliminated excuses for lateness or absences from work on personal business.

2. Work performance seems to be more efficient due to the reduction in the number of days lost through *alleged* illness and to the reduction in cost for a given output; these results are due to a more highly motivated work force and the need for less overtime working. (The usual gossip at the beginning and end of each day tends to be reduced, with employees arriving in a random manner and settling quietly down to work.) Furthermore, the system has created a quiet time—that is, the periods outside core time—when output can be more effective due to fewer interruptions.

3. There may be organizational improvements. For example, communications may improve as more precise instructions to subordinates tend to be necessary. Also the capital assets of a firm may be better used because of the larger total work period each day.

4. Flextime can be seen as a labor attraction. A reduction in labor turnover is likely because employees who are accustomed to a flexible system are less likely to be attracted to organizations that do not offer such a system. This appeal could lead to a reduction in recruitment and training costs.

5. Other factors that favor flextime: Basically, people want to work; when working conditions are right, employees willingly cooperate with management. Trust placed in a company's employees is repaid. Vir-

tually all organizations operating on flexible working hours claim that the working climate has been improved. Employees no longer see themselves as nine-to-five slaves but as responsible human beings; their commitment is increased and the organization benefits as a result.

Employee Advantages

1. Flextime allows employees to work according to their personal rhythms; some people are at their best first thing in the morning, while others are happier working later in the afternoon/evening. This flexibility tends to reduce the stress and strain of having to work fixed hours at predetermined times.

2. There is a better balance between private life and work. An individual has more opportunity to plan his or her free time and private life. People have more time for their families and their private time is much fuller and more satisfying. There is less reason for the sudden headache to see a special football game or an extra visit to the hairdresser, which in many cases leads to a guilty feeling, again putting pressure on the individual.

3. Travelling to and from work can be far less exhausting and harrowing as the rush hours can be avoided; the employee can arrive at work feeling much more relaxed. If a large number of workers in a large city begin to work on flextime schedules, the overall intensity of the rush-hour traffic will certainly decrease; traffic accident rates may also decline. Trends such as flextime may eventually lead to the elimination of the

traditional weekend, which would improve enormously the utilization of public resources and recreation facilities.

4. In many systems, the employee can amass credit hours, and the company may allow him to take a half-day or a whole day off in lieu. This advantage is clearly seen. However, it must once again be emphasized that time off during core time will be given only after consultation with the department head.

5. There are also economic advantages:

   • Travelling expenses may decrease by travelling at off-peak times.

   • Lateness and financial penalties disappear.

   • Many employees, through the nature of their jobs, have always expected to work additional time where necessary without extra pay. With flextime this additional time is credited.

Disadvantages/Problems

Management Disadvantages

1. Additional costs may arise from the need for time-recording equipment; no matter which system is adopted, some cost is incurred.

2. Administrative costs increase, but they can be controlled by leaving a good deal of the paper work to the employees themselves.

3. Overhead may increase as an office or factory will have to be open longer; heating, lighting and other such expenses will rise.

4. There may be some operational inconvenience because employees are not always present when required. Supervisory difficulties may occur, and additional supervisors may be required to cover the extra time bands. Communications may deteriorate as the fixed time when employees are obliged to be available is reduced, in some cases to four hours a day.

5. The problem of assuring safety and security also arises. A British company found that it would have safety problems in its laboratory; its flexible time is therefore limited since no one is allowed to carry out work of a dangerous nature alone in the laboratory.

6. There may also be miscellaneous disadvantages. Some workers may deliberately build up credit time by "staying over" for longer than the job demands. Friction may sometimes develop between employees who have the freedom of a flexible system and those who are excluded or restricted because of the job they do.

Employee Disadvantages

There may be some economic disadvantages. Overtime may be reduced because of more effective output. Productivity may rise but employees may not share the benefits of the increase. In some cases, personal absence privileges, such as for visits to the dentist or doctor, may be lost.

The introduction of flextime may also have some adverse effects on working conditions. For instance, the necessity for time-recording may be regarded as a decrease in status or another form of management control. The level of supervision may fall at the extremities of the day, and some employees may find that it is not available when required.

Further Reading

National Center for Productivity and Quality of Working Life, *Alternatives in the World of Work*. Washington, D.C., 1976.

ROBISON, DAVID, *Alternative Work Patterns*. Scarsdale, N.Y.: Work in America Institute, 1976.

7

Career Development

Company-sponsored *career development* programs offer
employees the opportunity to assess their skills and
capabilities, evaluate their career progress, and make plans
for furthering their personal career goals. These programs range from limited counseling services, through
formal seminars or workshops, to the use of various assessment techniques and diagnostic instruments.
Employees may work singly or in small groups, or both
ways, calling on the services of trained counselors or consultants in working out their plans. Many executives who
have instituted such programs seem to regard them not
only as worthwhile methods for improving the utilization

of human resources, but also as "benefit"-type programs that tend to attract and hold employees.

This discussion focuses on highly developed career development programs that have the formal commitment of top management and that offer thoroughgoing approaches to helping the employees work out their formal career plans.

A typical career development program is voluntary, it is oriented to the employee as an individual, and it protects the employee's right to the privacy of his or her own plan. Usually the personnel department or the department of human resources development operates the program. The employee's participation in the program begins with signing up for the next available program, whereupon he or she receives a package of self-assessment and self-study materials. Using these materials, the employee analyzes his or her present status, job functions, pay and other benefits, skills and capabilities, personal attitudes, and preferences for various kinds of work.

The employee may also have an opportunity to discuss the findings of this self-study process with a counsellor or human resources development specialist. Then the employee attends a workshop along with other employees, conducted by an experienced career development specialist. During this workshop, participants share ideas and experiences, compare views about working for the organization, and clarify their own individual career options. The workshop activities generally focus on goal-setting and on realistic planning. Employees learn about the resources offered by the organization, such as internal training programs, local educational programs sponsored on a tuition-reimbursement basis, new job opportunities within the organization, and developmental strategies that might fit their individual needs and goals.

As a result of the program, each participant has a better defined set of career goals, a plan for achieving them, and a better understanding of his or her strategy for making the next move.

Example

Wickes Corporation

The Wickes Corporation, a large furniture-manufacturing concern, conducts periodic career development programs, similar to the model program already described. A fairly elaborate package of diagnostic materials and assessment tools must be filled out and studied by the employee before attending the workshop. These materials include an individual personality profile, and a profile of the individual's current job, both of which help to identify significant areas of mismatch in performance or satisfaction.

Wickes' specialists also use a three-dimensional "strength-deployment" model, which helps the employee understand how he or she typically deals with people and situations, both conventionally and under pressure. In addition, the McClelland Social Motives model (dealing with the needs for achievement, power, and affiliation) help the employee and the counselor to understand the employee's personality better, insofar as it relates to career success.

The second stage of the Wickes program is a comprehensive three-day workshop, focused on personal development and goal-setting. With the help of the career development specialist, participants study their own findings, relate them to their jobs, and develop career goals that account for their values and personal needs. They then examine in detail the strategies for achieving these goals, and each one writes a personal plan. Wickes' management considers the career development program a valuable part of its human resource utilization strategy. By developing their people and by helping them to plan effective careers for themselves, they believe they can maximize their job effectiveness and automatically realize benefits in productivity and organizational performance.

Advantages

1. Career development programs can create a strong sense of identification with the organization on the part of the employees.

2. Employees who have stopped growing and developing can be motivated to renew themselves and take a new interest in their careers.

3. Developmental and training needs surface automatically, and the employee typically takes the initiative in approaching the manager in order to gain the necessary training and experience.

4. The self-assessment approach avoids feelings of defensiveness and rationalization processes characteristic of the standard performance-appraisal process.

5. Employee motivation and job effectiveness may increase, because many workers take a renewed interest

in their careers and decide to work harder for advancement to higher levels.

6. A career development program can identify and motivate people who have high potential for and interest in management jobs.

7. These benefits may manifest themselves in higher overall morale and improved social climate within the organization, with its attendant benefits of reduced absenteeism and turnover.

Disadvantages/Problems

1. Career development programs usually represent significant direct outlays of money and other direct costs, such as lost work time.

2. Costs may be a stumbling block to executive acceptance of the program, unless the executives already accept the premise that career development leads to improved employee effectiveness.

3. In an organization with a highly toxic social climate, a career development workshop—or any similar human-relations-oriented program—can open floodgates of employee animosity; previously repressed anger and hostility toward management may suddenly be released in destructive ways.

4. Some employees may decide—as a result of the workshop—that their career interests are best served by leaving the organization.

5. Managers who previously paid little attention to employee development must begin to work effectively with employees who have acquired much clearer goals and developed specific programs that affect their day-to-day relationships with their supervisors.

Further Reading

FLIPPO, EDWIN, *Principles of Personnel Management.* New York: McGraw-Hill Book Co., 1976.

WEILER, NICHOLAS W., *Reality and Career Planning.* Reading, Mass.: Addison-Wesley, 1977.

8

Problem Counseling

Employees with severe personal problems or adjustment difficulties can, in some organizations, get assistance in the form of *problem counseling* by experienced professionals. Organizational approaches to problem counseling involve in-house staff people, referral to and cooperation with community helping resources, and combinations of these two approaches. This form of support is becoming more prevalent as an employee service, as more and more people experience difficulties due to life-stress caused by various upheavals in their lives. Executives who have implemented such programs seem to look upon them as reasonable investments in maintaining not only the effectiveness of their organizations' human resources, but also a generally positive social value completely apart from economic benefits.

The kinds of problems that create the need for problem counseling include:

1. alcoholism,
2. drug abuse,
3. psychiatric disorders,
4. general adjustment difficulties,
5. stress-related emotional and physical problems,
6. difficulties in relationships with one's superior,
7. some forms of personal legal difficulties, and
8. health difficulties.

The aim of a problem counseling program is to restore the employee to a fully functional status, in which his or her work performance is no longer jeopardized by the personal problem. Organizations vary in the extent of the services they offer and in the extent to which the helping professionals get involved in the personal lives of the employees who experience the problems. Usually the criterion for determining the appropriate level and extent of problem assistance is the employee's job performance. For example, an employee with a drinking problem who nevertheless carries out his or her job duties satisfactorily will generally not be involved in such a program. Very few alcoholics are willing to concede the severity of their problems, and consequently they do not seek professional help. However, if the alcoholism seriously interferes with job performance, the employee may be offered problem counseling services as part of a probationary program in preference to summary dismissal.

Some organizations invest more substantially in problem counseling, and in these cases almost any employee who has a problem severe enough to motivate him or her to seek help can get it. A typical approach for medium and large organizations is to maintain a small professional staff of "trouble shooters," who can work with distressed employees on a small scale using organizational funds and resources and who help those with more substantial problems find the necessary community resources to get their problems solved. Sometimes merely helping a distraught employee find an attorney may suffice. In other cases, putting the person in touch with an appropriate government agency may help. Experienced helping professionals can often help the employee locate community resources that are available at no charge.

Examples

Kennecott Copper Corporation

Kennecott Copper Corporation in Salt Lake City, Utah, pioneered one of the first and most enlightened problem counseling programs in the country. What began in 1969 as an alcoholism rehabilitation program grew into a full-scale effort to help employees with personal problems of all kinds. Helping professionals on the staff of Kennecott concluded that contemporary alcohol and drug

rehabilitation programs were severely limited in effectiveness due to the automatic stigmatization of the troubled
individuals who took advantage of them. Most troubled
individuals, they believed, would not take advantage of the
programs except as a last resort, to avoid the social stigma
associated with drinking and drug abuse.
They redefined the program as one of general
employee assistance, with absolute confidentiality guaran-
teed. Employees could dial a certain telephone number,
coded to spell INSIGHT, describe their needs, and receive
brief advice or referral to a community service agency,
without disclosing their identity. They could also make
confidential appointments with staff professionals for
more extensive assistance. One counselor commented:
"We help people name kids, handle adoptions, get kidney
dialysis machines, deal with deterioration and death of a
cancer-stricken family member, resolve disputes with land-
lords, and untangle all the problems caused by hit and run
accidents." Other activities include crisis counseling in
cases of potential suicide, help with marital difficulties,
and financial emergencies.

Staff counselors built strong cooperative relationships
with community mental health organizations, hospitals,
family service agencies, and legal assistance organizations.

Other Cases

Problem counseling programs exist or are under development at other large organizations. Control Data Corporation in Minneapolis employs eighteen full-time and
four part-time professional counselors. CDC management
considers the program extremely worthwhile and feels

that measurable dollar savings nearly offset program costs, not to mention the social benefits involved. Helping professionals involved in the program also believe that many nonquantifiable benefits accrue to the company, through increased personal effectiveness and higher morale among those who have received help from the service.

TRW, Inc., in Redondo Beach, California, also has a staff counseling service for general employee use. In addition, these professionals train first-line supervisors in the skills of "emotional first aid," to enable them to give preliminary assistance and support to employees who experience crises on the job.

As a result of increasing interest on the part of large companies in helping employees deal with their problems, at least one service consortium has been established to serve a group of companies including General Electric, Bell Telephone, and Scott Paper, as well as a bank and an insurance company. With the help of a grant from the Department of Health, Education and Welfare, the organization provides counseling and crisis intervention services to client organizations on a direct-reimbursement basis. With the enthusiastic cooperation of community service agencies as well as the sponsoring organizations themselves, this concept may well spread to other areas and other organizations.

Advantages

Clearly, programs in problem counseling contribute to the mental health and well-being of employees, and they frequently remove obstacles to personal and work effectiveness. These general features may translate into such specific benefits as:

1. more rapid solutions to personal problems and speedier recovery from personal adjustment difficulties, with the help of experienced professional counselors,

2. less lost time from work due to dealing with problems and suffering from their side effects,

3. a possible reduction in stress-induced illness connected with personal problems,

4. fewer terminations for inadequate job performance and consequently lower costs for replacement,

5. fewer disciplinary problems, due to the effectiveness of staff counselors in getting to the causes of performance problems in cases where employees seek assistance,

6. improved morale and more enthusiastic job performance on the part of troubled employees who have been helped to overcome their difficulties, and

7. reduced impact on co-workers and supervisors, due to more rapid and direct solutions to personal problems.

Disadvantages/Problems

1. Problem counseling programs inevitably require direct outlays of funds for start-up, maintenance, and follow-through.

2. Traditionally oriented managers may undermine the effectiveness of the program, on the conviction that the organization should not become involved in the personal lives of its employees.

3. Executives who require that all socially oriented programs show proven cost savings in prior analysis may fail to appreciate the broad-scale effects of nonfinancial benefits.

Further Reading

CATHEY, PAUL, "Solving Workers' Problems: Industry Tries New Approach," *Iron Age* (October 17, 1977), p. 27.

9

Stress-Reduction Training

Stress-reduction training is a form of individualized personal development training that imparts specific skills helpful to employees and managers in eliminating, reducing, or avoiding emotionally induced stress. *Stress* is defined from the medical point of view as a physical arousal process within the human body, triggered by emotional reactions to pressure, conflict, or various forms of upheaval in an individual's life and work situations. The physical stress response, or *stress syndrome*, is characterized by a distinctive pattern of excitation of the person's *sympathetic nervous system*, together with an increased secretion of certain hormones, particularly adrenaline.

Although the stress response can result from physical traumas, such as injuries, bacterial infections, excessive heat or cold, high noise levels, and the like, stress-reduction training is concerned with stress that arises from the individual's emotional responses to a demanding or troublesome environment. As Dr. Hans Selye, the originator of the concept of the stress syndrome has pointed out, stress in and of itself is a normal reaction of the human body. It is only when the individual experiences prolonged high levels of stress, without relief, that normal stress becomes "distress." In fact, Selye uses the term *eustress* to differentiate the stress associated with challenging and rewarding activities, which the healthy, well-adjusted person can deal with adequately, from the distress levels associated with the overloading and loss of one's feelings of adequacy and security.

Stress-defense skills include the neurological skill of *deep relaxation,* which helps to condition and restore the individual's nervous system, making it easier for him or her to remain relatively relaxed and calm in pressure situations. Deep relaxation practice also seems to bring about a variety of beneficial effects on overall health and well-being. These training techniques include the simple one of progressive muscle relaxation, as well as the more sophisticated methods of self-hypnosis, meditation, and *autogenic training*—a technique developed in Germany in the 1940s. Biofeedback techniques are also becoming increasingly popular for relaxation training.

Related stress-defense skills include techniques for self-management in problem situations and for lifestyle redesign to minimize or eliminate unnecessary sources of pressure and consequent stress.

The problem of occupational stress has increased dramatically during the post-war period, and the stress of

American life in general has been increasing at an alarming rate. Stress has been shown to play an important and frequently decisive part in heart disease, now the principal cause of death in America. More Americans die from heart attacks and other heart diseases than from all other causes combined. Some researchers have even claimed that cancer, the number two cause of death in America, frequently has an element of stress in its origins. The third-place killer, stroke, is also closely linked with chronic high levels of stress.

Stress is also known to aggravate a variety of other diseases, most notably diabetes. In addition, many people suffer from minor health disorders such as digestive upsets, ulcers, chronic headaches, fatigue, sleeping problems, and sexual dysfunction brought on by sustained high levels of anxiety without relaxation and neurological recuperation.

The National Institute of Occupational Safety and Health now has a special staff unit to study the problems of occupational stress. NIOSH studies have identified a number of occupations that induce unusually high levels of stress in workers. Many of these jobs, ironically, are in the health services field and in the helping professions. Welfare case workers, physicians, nurses, nurses' aides, and psychiatrists all seem to experience much higher levels of continued stress than laborers, clerical workers, and college professors. Air traffic controllers seem to suffer the most. Workers at machine-paced jobs also seem to have difficulty with stress build-up.

Organizations experience the direct cost impacts of chronic stress in their employees, through health problems that lead to decreased work performance, absenteeism, and turnover. Escapist behavior such as alcoholism, drug abuse, and tranquilizer dependency tends to compound the problems by diminishing the overall quality of life for individuals who suffer from chronic stress.

Stress-reduction training is a very new concept at this time, and it has so far been evaluated only in small-scale situations. It can be seen as a component of an organizational development strategy, aimed at reducing environmentally induced stress as well as the individual's personal level of reactivity.

Examples

Department of Public Welfare

The Department of Public Welfare in San Diego County, California, instituted a program of stress-reduction training to counteract the increasing effects of job-related stress on eligibility workers who dealt with large numbers of welfare clients each day. Not only were many of DPW's clients in extreme distress, but they also often lacked the conventional social skills to make their transactions with the workers proceed smoothly. These distressed individuals lived outside the mainstream of conventional society and often had personal adjustment problems and culturally related self-limiting attitudes and habits. They therefore frequently used the workers as targets for their frustration and hostility.

Eligibility workers (EWs) reported feeling overloaded, rushed, beleaguered, and chronically tense. They felt helpless to overcome many of the problems facing their clients, and they also felt anxious about the high production schedules for processing client cases. They frequently described feelings of inadequacy and lack of control. An increasing number of them reported health problems, ranging from fatigue and sleeplessness to sexual dysfunction and nervous breakdown. At least one case of suicide was thought to be affected by high levels of chronic stress. In addition, morale at the working levels of the organization declined to extremely low levels, and interpersonal relationships within and between work units degenerated severely.

The training staff decided to set up a pilot program in stress-reduction training for the EWs. Two specially trained instructors prepared a two-day workshop for a group of thirty workers. During the workshop, the instructors helped the EWs to reassess their job situations, to reexamine their own feelings about the job, and to revise their attitudes about the effects of their jobs on their lives and health.

Participants learned the skills of deep relaxation, self-management, and lifestyle redesign, applying them to their overall life situations with the job as a special area of focus. Virtually all of them discovered ways to increase their feelings of security and adequacy during the working day; they were able to adopt strategies for dealing with problem situations that gave them a stronger sense of efficacy and control.

Feedback from the participants was more enthusiastic and positive than or any other training program the department had conducted. Morale among the trainees soared, at least in the short term. Trainees who had been through the training program together felt a special sort of camaraderie, and tended to support one another and to spread the word about stress-reduction strategies to the co-workers. The training staff received many requests to repeat the training workshop, and a waiting list quickly developed for attendance at the next one. After several repeats of the program, department trainers reported unprecedented employee support and enthusiasm for stress-reduction training: A number of employees felt the training had given them coping skills that made their entire lives more effective and fulfilling. Almost all attendees reported improved capabilities for handling their jobs, and a number of supervisors confirmed these claims.

The Welfare Department has apparently made stress-reduction training a regular part of its human resources development program.

Managing on-the-job Stress

Management interest in the problem of stress and in stress-reduction training is increasing rapidly. At the University of California extensions in San Diego, Riverside, Irvine, and Santa Cruz, Dr. Karl Albrecht has developed a program titled "Managing on-the-job Stress." This one-day seminar has been attended by business executives, welfare managers and workers, law enforcement people, doctors, nurses, attorneys and psychiatrists, as well as a variety of other kinds of workers.

Other human resources development consultants and industrial trainers are developing training programs and materials for stress-reduction training. This concept may become one of the more significant advances in human resources development, and it may well pave the way for the long-awaited "humanization" of our American business organizations.

Advantages

Stress-reduction training develops and encourages the whole person to think about his or her entire life. Consequently, it enables the individual to become more effective in a variety of ways, including at work. The wide application of stress-reduction training, coupled with programs aimed at improving the organizational climate, may turn out to be one of the most powerful management strategies for improving the effectiveness and utilization of human resources. A more effective work force offers such benefits to the organization as:

1. a higher level of overall health and well-being, thereby reducing the costs of health benefit programs,

2. less lost time due to sickness and stress-related absences,

3. lower turnover due to a more rewarding social climate within the organization,

4. generally higher morale and improved working relationships among employees and between employees and supervisors,

5. higher productivity due to increased worker effectiveness, and

6. higher-quality work in areas such as customer and client service.

Disadvantages/Problems

1. Direct costs for training programs can be substantial for organizations with large numbers of people.

2. Unconventional training techniques, such as deep relaxation, sometimes meet with suspicion or skepticism from managers who know little about stress physiology or who have traditionalist attitudes about training programs that are beneficial to employees in ways not restricted directly to their jobs.

3. Employees who learn better self-management skills sometimes react assertively against oppressive "rat race" work conditions, or they otherwise take action against highly stressful jobs. Some may even resign from highly stressful jobs as part of redesigning their lifestyles; managers need to be able to cope with these reactions honestly and constructively.

Further Reading

ALBRECHT, KARL, *Stress and the Manager.* Englewood Cliffs, N.J.: Prentice-Hall, Inc., 1978.

LAMOTT, KENNETH, *Escape from Stress.* New York: Berkeley Medallion, 1975.

SELYE, HANS, *The Stress of Life.* New York: McGraw-Hill Book Company, 1956.

————*Stress Without Distress.* New York: Signet, 1975.

10

Assertive Communication Training

Assertive communication training enables employees and managers to deal with one another, and with customers and clients when necessary, in straightforward ways that recognize the rights and needs of all the individuals involved. Pioneered by Dr. Manuel Smith and other psychologists, assertive communication training provides certain specific verbal skills the employee can use to avoid being intimidated or manipulated by others.

This concept arose from the recognition that virtually everybody has defensive feelings, learned early in life, that can sometimes come into play at inappropriate times. These defensive feelings often lead a person to give in to the intimidating behavior of others, to accept situations or make agreements that the person knows are detrimental to his or her own interests, and to negotiate ineffectively. Assertive communication techniques are essentially verbal strategies, coupled with revised attitudes about one's self and one's self-esteem.

Assertive training differentiates very carefully between *assertive behavior,* which is seen as constructive, and *aggressive behavior,* which is seen as anti-social and detrimental to one's own interests in the long run. Whereas an aggressive approach to dealing with another person—an irate customer, for example—involves a "win–lose" mentality, an assertive approach involves finding a balance of the two transacting personalities, with respect for the interests of each and with a workable compromise as the espoused goal of the transaction.

Two individuals can communicate and solve problems together much more effectively if both of them understand and can use assertive techniques. However, even if only one of them understands the concept, he can still do a great deal to steer the transaction along a constructive course, even if the other person is upset, angry, or aggressive.

The basic assumption behind assertive communication is that one's self-esteem does not need to come into jeopardy in dealing with others, even if they lack the skill or consideration to approach the transaction constructively. A person can only be manipulated by others, for example, if he or she lets ancient guilt feelings come into play when the other person makes a statement intended to "hook" into such feelings. High pressure sales people often do this. People asking unreasonable favors often use the same tactics. Other forms of manipulation involve the use of accusations, leading or loaded questions, sidetracking the conversation with irrelevant diversions, and questioning one's honesty or integrity.

If one can learn to develop a high level of self-esteem and to separate one's feelings of self-worth from the nature of the transaction at hand, then the other person has a much more difficult time intimidating or manipulating him. And since aggressive interpersonal strategies— "pushiness"—are such a common part of the American social armamentarium, this dissociation technique is a highly valuable everyday skill.

In an assertive communication workshop, participants learn the basic concepts of self-esteem, together with verbal techniques such as:

1. *Broken record*—calmly repeating what one wants, while refusing to get sidetracked by diversions or manipulative techniques used by others.

2. *Fogging*—refusing to put up a tangible defense against accusative or critical remarks, by calmly acknowledging the possibility that the other person's criticisms *may* be true or justified, but sticking to the main point of the conversation.

3. *Free information*—offering facts about one's self or what one knows to another, to promote the free and constructive exchange of information.

4. *Negative assertion*—calmly agreeing with, and even amplifying critical remarks made about one's self by others; declining to fall back into conventional defensive tactics of apology, evasion, or counterattack.

5. *Negative inquiry*—calmly prompting the other person to continue giving criticisms of one's self, drawing out and exhausting manipulative criticism, asking for specific feedback on negative aspects of one's self, without adopting a defensive or hostile role.

6. *Self-disclosure*—telling the other person about one's thoughts or feelings in such a way as to add valuable information to the exchange and to foster an honest, straightforward, interpersonal transaction.

7. *Workable compromise*—bargaining for a course of action that balances the interests of both parties and that especially does not place one in a position of feeling defeated, manipulated, or "taken"; settling for a compromise based on its intrinsic value, rather than on the basis of the aggressiveness and social skill of the other person.

A typical workshop training program gives participants an opportunity not only to understand and discuss the key concepts and techniques but also to put them into practice under controlled circumstances. The aim of the training is to enable participants to use the verbal techniques naturally and easily in pressure or difficult situations that arise in their jobs. In a sense, assertive skills are a category of general purpose social skills, which tend to enhance the effectiveness of the individual in almost any business situation involving transactions with others.

Examples

A large number of organizations have used assertive communication training to help employees handle their jobs better and to improve their mutual relationships.

United States Navy

A United States Navy laboratory put most of its staff of scientists and other technical professionals through a training program in assertive communication. Executives there report that the participants developed greater interpersonal skills and learned to deal with one another more effectively in discussion and problem-solving situations involving complex issues. Also, the combination of a strong scientific and logical background with improved social skills increased the potential of many members of the staff for advancement to management positions.

A Small College

The Dean of a small community college adult education center, together with his office staff, studied assertive communication techniques to improve their cooperation and effectiveness in hectic situations, especially during rush periods at the beginning and end of each academic term. Several members of the staff were more able to keep their tempers better in pressure situations, as a result of having more powerful strategies for problem-solving and conflict resolution. As an added benefit, the increased use of assertive skills also led to an increased self-awareness of aggressive behaviors on the part of various staff members. These members learned to monitor their own reactions more accurately and to adopt more constructive approaches to dealing with one another, even in "panic" situations.

Advantages

1. Customer-contact employees function more effectively, alienating fewer customers and maintaining a positive company image.

2. Assertive employees experience much lower levels of job-related stress, because they feel a greater sense of potency and they experience fewer strong emotions in their job situations.

3. Managers learn to deal with employees in more open, straightforward ways, deploying their formal authority gracefully and sparingly.

4. Formerly shy employees who often have good ideas develop greater confidence in themselves and express their ideas more forcefully.

5. Morale and social climate generally improve in a work unit after its members have been trained collectively in assertive communication techniques.

6. Employees may take greater initiative and innovate more, as a result of increased confidence in their ability to promote and defend their ideas.

Disadvantages/Problems

1. The quality of the learning process depends heavily on the maturity, insight, and assertive skills of the instructor who leads the training seminar. Immature

and poorly trained instructors, particularly in women's programs, have sometimes mistaken aggressive techniques for assertive techniques and have led participants to adopt counterproductive strategies oriented to win–lose transacting styles.

2. Participants must be cautioned not to expect all their communication problems to vanish as a result of assertive training; they must still deal occasionally with individuals who are extremely immature, unreasonable, or unwilling to transact honestly and in good faith.

3. Aggressive individuals sometimes select specific techniques from the assertive repertoire without changing their attitudes about dealing with others; they may simply become more cleverly aggressive, without grasping the significance of the basic concepts that form the foundation for the techniques.

Further Reading

DYER, DR. WAYNE W., *Your Erroneous Zones*. New York: Avon, 1976.

SMITH, MANUEL J., *When I Say No, I Feel Guilty*. New York: Bantam Books, 1975

11

Transactional Analysis (TA)

Transactional analysis (TA) has rapidly become a popular system of practical psychology that enables most people to understand and deal with normal human behavior more effectively. First developed by Eric Berne as a system to help psychiatric patients think and talk about their difficulties, it quickly found its way into the popular literature and became "everyman's psychology." Many management consultants and writers have adapted the concepts and terminology of TA to the kinds of activities that go on in the business world, and the system is becoming increasingly popular as an adjunct to management training and to various kinds of employee training.

The remarkable popularity of TA in business organizations as a layman's psychology stems from two factors:

First is the ever-increasing need on the part of executives and managers to understand human behavior and to deal with it explicitly as part of the job of managing. The enormous changes in American attitudes and institutions since the Second World War have drawn management attention increasingly away from the purely technical approach and toward a more humanistic approach. Many senior executives and middle managers are chagrined to discover how much they don't know about human behavior, particularly in the area of motivation and job satisfaction; and they are pleased to find out how much valuable information is available from the applied behavioral sciences. Practicing managers have developed a remarkable appetite for practical, useful models and concepts for dealing with the diversity of normal human behavior in the work situation.

The *second* factor is TA's charming simplicity. Although it has distinct limitations as a behavioral model and should therefore not be taken as the ultimate psychological system, it captures some of the most important features of the two-person face-to-face communication interaction. As such it covers a great portion of everyday human experience. Managers and employees alike can learn the basic concepts and terminology of TA either by reading one or more of the excellent books available or by attending a training seminar. Equipped with the basic two-person TA model and a few of the related concepts and terms, a person can routinely analyze communication situations and work out ways to deal with them more effectively.

This chapter simply provides a general understanding of TA's applications as a tool for thinking and communicating. Readers interested in pursuing the concepts in depth will probably want to study one of the many books now available, some of which are listed at the end of this chapter. Accordingly, the following discussion simply summarizes the basic structure of the TA model.

TA conceives of each person as transacting with other people in comparatively patterned ways. Each person, according to the theory, can adopt one of three distinct personality patterns, or *ego states*, according to the situation and his or her own personal make-up. These three ego states are the Parent, the Adult, and the Child. The terms are capitalized to call attention to their somewhat specialized definitions.

When in the *Adult* ego state, a person engages in primarily cognitive and rational processes, such as stating facts, questioning, observing, comparing, deciding, and exchanging information with others. In this state, no strong feelings are evident, and the person is in a "data-processing" mode.

In the *Child* ego state, the person's behavior is dominated by relatively strong feelings, either positive or negative. Thus, even when a grown-up person is feeling happy, sad, playful, angry, or frightened he is said to be in his Child state in TA terminology. The Child state is just as normal and valuable a part of one's functioning as the Adult state. The term Child does *not* have the connotation of immaturity or inadequacy when used within the TA model.

When in the *Parent* ego state, the person typically simulates authority-oriented behavior he or she observed on the part of those grown-up people who served as primary role-models during early life. In transacting from the Parent state, the person draws upon values, beliefs, basic "truths" (some of which may not be true but are taken as true), and rules for living learned many years ago from the natural parents and other significant grown-up people who raised and socialized with the person when he or she was small. Each person's Parent state serves as a "reference library" for information about how to live; and the behavior of someone who is in the Parent state will be characteristically influenced by the archaic stored data upon which the person draws.

To grow and develop personally the individual must learn to identify these three ego states, to understand how they function, and to keep them simultaneously separated but integrated in a flexible pattern of thinking, reacting, and behaving. TA doctrine calls for the Adult state to function as the "executive" state, with the individual occasionally moving into the Parent or Child state as the situation warrants.

Skill at communicating, from the TA point of view, involves the ability to observe one's self and others while transacting, to classify the various ego states involved, to determine the patterns that characterize the transaction, and to adapt one's behavior intelligently to manage the transaction effectively. The fundamental transactional unit is known as a *stroke,* which in its simplest form is merely a message of some kind that acknowledges another person's existence. Other kinds of messages are progressively more complex and symbolic. A transactional stimulus from one person—that is, a statement or an action—elicits a response from the other person and vice versa. A sequence of these interchanges becomes a communication transaction, which can be analyzed with the aid of the Parent–Adult–Child model.

A training workshop in TA includes exploration of the basic Parent–Adult–Child model and its underlying concepts; it also involves a great deal of practical experience, role-playing, and analysis exercises to help participants make the basic skills facile and natural. When used as a group training approach, such as part of a team-building program, TA gives co-workers and managers a common framework and a common vocabulary for talking about how they get along with one another.

Examples

TA, as a training approach and as a training tool, has had many organizational applications. In most cases, TA is one of a variety of approaches, and seldom has an organization adopted it as a formal method having anything to do with its regular management practice. Consequently, no extensive "organizational" examples are offered here. However, the majority of large business organizations in the country have applied the approach to some extent and in some areas of their structures.

A major airline, for example, designed a training program for customer-contact employees based on TA principles, titled "TACT"—Transactional Analysis for Customer-contact Training. Contact employees learned to analyze their transactions with customers, to identify the operating ego states, and to detect the problem cues in difficult situations. They learned to deal effectively with customers who were distraught, confused, bewildered, frightened, or angry—and to manage the ego states involved more effectively. Techniques emphasized helping the disturbed customer return to a rational, cooperative Adult state, after which business can proceed constructively. Airline executives feel the program has a number of benefits, including higher employee morale and lower job stress, as well as improved customer relations and more repeat business.

Advantages

1. The TA system is simple, easy to learn, and easy to apply.

2. It focuses on the kinds of behavioral situations managers and employees enounter most—the two-person face-to-face communication situation.

3. The concepts are somewhat "contagious"; the simple terminology helps a TA-trained person to impart some of the key ideas of the system to others who are not familiar with it.

4. The concepts and techniques tend to carry over into the private lives of individuals who learn the system, making them generally happier and more effective in a variety of ways.

5. The general use of TA techniques within a work unit, especially when encouraged by a manager who understands and uses them, tends to increase morale and improve the social climate within the group.

6. Managers who learn to apply the TA model become much more perceptive of the ego states of their employees in various situations, and they tend to become much more aware of the part they can play in motivating employees through positive treatment.

Disadvantages/Problems

1. Some people may become so fascinated with the model that they tend to overuse it, failing to recognize its limitations.

2. Because the model is simplistic—its primary advantage—it covers only certain selected aspects of behavior; a manager interested in human behavior should learn a variety of models and concepts so as to have a balanced view.

3. Some people may merely pick up a few key terms and slogans without bothering to learn the basic concepts of the TA model, and they may use their superficial knowledge to simulate more sophistication and psychological expertise than they really have.

Further Reading

BOSHEAR, WALTON C., and KARL G. ALBRECHT, *Understanding People: Models and Concepts*. La Jolla, Calif.: University Associates, 1977.

JAMES, MURIEL, and DOROTHY JONGEWARD, *Born to Win*. Reading, Mass.: Addison-Wesley, 1971.

JAMES, MURIEL, *The OK Boss*. Reading, Mass.: Addison-Wesley, 1975.

MEININGER, JUT, *Success Through Transactional Analysis*. New York: Signet, 1973.

Section Two

ORGANIZATIONAL NEEDS

This section concentrates on developments aimed at maximizing the contribution of labor in the achievement of organizational needs. Such developments have arisen because labor is no longer a cheap resource and therefore needs to be used in the most efficient manner.

12

Human Resources Planning

Human resources planning is the systematic process of analyzing an organization's present make-up in terms of the different categories of people within its work force, analyzing its future needs for people based on business or operational projections, and determining how to meet those needs by recruitment and development. Though such planning does not provide a rigid forecast, it is a guideline to understanding factors influencing the make-up of the work force. It also provides notes on future developments. In the long run it deals with the labor force as a whole rather than with the career patterns of individuals. Briefly, it is concerned with the best use of one of the organization's most expensive assets, its people.

Human resources planning can therefore be viewed as a strategy for developing and maintaining "human capital," just as effectively as the organization develops and maintains its traditional forms of capital. Until quite recently great attention had been given to the planning and use of money and matériel but little to the costing and effective use of labor. As labor costs continue to rise, as work becomes progressively more knowledge-oriented and complex, and as the composition of the American work force changes, more organizations are developing conscious policies and methods for human resources planning.

In many cases this planning relies on the use of computer models. In simple terms a model can be constructed that divides the various grades of employees into categories; these categories are then linked with age structure. The numbers of people at each level and in each age group are fed into these computerized "boxes"; this gives the initial "stock." All this information is available from employee records. The computer then "wastes off" this initial stock by taking into account prediction factors such as promotion, turnover, retirement, and death. Then the computer report shows probable gaps and areas where more people will have to be recruited. This process is then repeated for each successive year, extending the computer estimates from one year to the next, thus estimating future demand. For each year, union negotiations and management decisions on recruitment and promotion policy have to be included in the computer analysis, as these affect needs in successive years.

This forecasting model can also be used to predict the future basis for management strength, by identifying the number of high-potential individuals of various ages and specialties who may be considered eligible for development and promotion.

Projecting future demand is a difficult task. It requires the projection of future growth, productivity, technological and production changes at both national and local levels, of shifts in the work force, and of any changes in government legislation. The analysis has to consider carefully four primary areas of change: technological, social, economic, and political.

Technological changes that have immediate effects on human resources, in terms of occupation and skills, arise from changes in energy, materials, and technical systems. The major types of social change that affect the composition of the work force are population trends, education, and social mobility. A general pattern of economic growth is interrelated with technological and social change. The rate of economic development is influenced, in turn, by political change. Three major areas of political change affect a business's labor requirements: foreign policy, legislation pertaining to wage and salary policy, and monetary policy.

Once the macro and micro factors have been considered, human resource planners can formulate a plan ensuring effective acquisition and utilization of labor resources.

Computerizing the planning model has the important advantage of flexibility in testing various assumptions about the future. Once the model is available, personnel planners can try various assumptions about future demand. The computer can rapidly recalculate the differences and present a series of output reports, each showing the effects of a different assumption. This capability gives a manager a good idea of the relative sensitivity of the planning figures to uncertainties in the forecasts.

Example

Wismer and Becker Corporation

Wismer and Becker Corporation, a construction contracting company in California, has developed a human resources forecasting and planning system, supported by a very progressive approach to periodic job evaluation, employee assessment, and career guidance.

The comparatively small company uses a graphic planning system, based on a color-coded organization chart showing every position in the organization. W&M managers refer to this as a manpower map. It shows each individual in each job slot, and it is coded to show each person's evaluational status. Four levels—ready-for-immediate-upgrade, stay-put, caution, and misfit—tell the current status of the incumbent.

The company also uses a periodic opinion survey, or "morale audit," by means of which it assesses the general social climate in the organization. Planners also use basic demographic data, forecasting figures for the construction industry, and operations planning figures to keep a current situation estimate for human resources. Personnel specialists base recruiting and hiring plans on the human resources planning model.

Advantages

1. With human resources planning, an organization can recruit the right number of people at the entry levels as well as remove people from a top-heavy structure.

2. Managers can move people from overstaffed areas to those with too few people; annual appraisals can help to indicate potential for movement to other areas.

3. Human resources planning helps to show the implications of early retirement policy and of changes in recruitment and promotion plans.

4. It shows which age group is likely to be most stable in terms of employment.

5. It highlights areas of high wastage; planners can then do an in-depth study to determine why recruitment is difficult in those areas.

Disadvantages/Problems

1. Human resources planning can only highlight gaps. It cannot say *how* one ought to recruit staff, and it cannot solve surrounding environmental problems of recruitment.

2. It must reflect all environmental changes that can lead to difficulties.

3. It is difficult to predict future technological and production changes; rapid changes in government policy can also create difficulties in this area.

4. The paperwork required may be relatively expensive, especially for the smaller organization.

Further Reading

BRAHAM, J. T., *Practical Manpower Planning*. London: Institute of Personnel Management, 1975.

FLIPPO, EDWIN, *Principles of Personnel Management*. New York: McGraw-Hill Book Company, 1976.

LYNCH, J. J., *Making Manpower Effective*. London: Pan, 1968.

SCHEIN, EDGAR, "Why Is Human Resource Planning and Development Important?" *Behavioral Sciences Newsletter* (December 12, 1977).

13

Scanlon Plan

The *Scanlon Plan* is a cooperative program in which labor and management progressively increase productivity while maintaining job security and distributing part of the cost savings back to the employees in the form of productivity bonuses. The concept is usually attributed to management consultant Joseph Scanlon, who experimented extensively with productivity improvement techniques in the late 1940s and 1950s.

The Scanlon Plan requires three key elements to work effectively:

1. a basic philosphy of cooperative action between workers and managers,

2. a system for collecting and acting on employee suggestions for operational improvements that can increase productivity, and

3. a formula that prescribes the way in which extra revenue due to increased productivity will be shared with the members of the work force.

Such a program begins with an initial productivity measure, or base ratio, that serves as a benchmark for assessing the benefits of improvements. Using current-year accounting data, analysts determine the fraction of sales volume required to pay labor costs. This ratio of labor dollars to revenue dollars becomes a key variable in the planning process.

Presumably, if employees can develop operational improvements that increase the next year's production output and consequently sales income, then they will collectively receive a bonus for that year equal to the labor ratio multiplied by the increase in sales. In this way, the organization receives extra profit roughly equal to the previous margin, and the employees receive the equivalent of a pay raise for having achieved the higher levels of performance. If the improvements continue to sustain productivity levels in following years, then the bonus continues during those years. If additional productivity increases occur through employee suggestions, the additional revenue increases also become available as bonus income, according to the same ratio.

Example

DeSoto

Probably the best-known and most extensively studied Scanlon Plan application is in DeSoto, Incorporated, a Texas company that manufactures paints and other chemical coatings. DeSoto instituted the plan in 1971, after a careful study of its possibilities. With about three hundred employees and gross sales of over $200 million, DeSoto is not a highly labor-intensive operation. However, managers felt that employee-initiated improvements could still produce some substantial increases in production output, especially in the areas of process redesign and modification of equipment and facilities. The plan was undertaken after management agreement and a secret ballot among the employees.

DeSoto instituted the Scanlon Plan in one of its four plants in 1971, and favorable results led to the extension of the program to each of the other plants in the next three years respectively. Improvement suggestions yielded an increase over the 1970 output rate, in gallons per hour, of 28 percent by 1972 and 41 percent by 1973. Although labor costs per gallon increased as a result of the bonus paid for the increased production, the total cost per gallon actually declined as a result of the greater production efficiency. Employees and managers alike considered the plan a very successful one.

DeSoto employees, including managers, received bonus pay in proportion to their individual salaries. Bonuses ranged from 4 percent to 7 percent over the first three years of the plan's operation. Employees received bonus payments on a monthly basis, according to accounting department calculations of labor costs and total production.

Advantages

In a successful Scanlon Plan application, both the company and the employees benefit jointly. The performance measure of dollars of revenue per dollar of labor becomes a matter of interest to both. Whereas an employee may ordinarily be indifferent to cost savings, on the basis that his or her suggestion would merely transfer funds from the company's cost account to its profit account, the productivity bonus leads a worker to see it as transferring money from an expense item into a shared profit between himself and the company. This automatically stimulates a greater interest and sense of involvement in productivity. Other advantages include:

1. Employees and managers tend to cooperate more extensively on a day-to-day basis, as a result of having a common personal interest in efficiency.

2. Morale may improve substantially as a result of the feelings of involvement and efficacy the employees gain from being listened to.

3. Counterproductive behaviors—such as carelessness leading to waste and product spoilage or improper maintenance and handling of machines—may decline

as employees try consistently and even unconsciously to keep production at high levels.

4. A great deal of the traditional labor–management animosity may be eliminated; time standards tend to give way to more comprehensive measures of productivity.

5. Turnover may decline substantially, as employees may be able to earn more in a Scanlon Plan company than in other companies.

6. The suggestion system used in the Scanlon Plan can pave the way for other forms of participative management and employee involvement in improving the effectiveness of the organization.

Disadvantages/Problems

1. Calculating the labor ratio and establishing the means for distributing productivity bonuses may be a complex process, requiring the skills of the accountant; employees must accept management's figures on faith.

2. Managers may be reluctant to abandon traditional time-study methods and to accept the notion that employees will work to keep production levels high.

3. Managers may resent distributing extra profits to employees which might actually be attributable to quirks in the marketplace, technological advances, or

effective managerial action; traditional managers may see these extra profits as "theirs" to use as they see fit.

4. If the existing relationship between management and the labor union is highly abrasive and distrustful, they will not likely be able to reach an agreement on the key variables of the Plan; old feuds and animosities may scuttle the program before it begins to show positive results.

5. Some labor leaders have a strong personal stake in continuing adversary relations with the management group. They may sense that a Scanlon Plan can improve employee attitudes toward management, a development which they consider a threat to their own roles.

6. Seldom can successive productivity increases be achieved for an indefinite period; sooner or later, good ideas tend to run out. Although bonus pay will continue for previous accomplishments, employees may eventually come to take the bonus system for granted. Consequently, its value as a morale and attitude factor is probably temporary.

7. Uncontrollable factors in the business environment may defeat the economic advantages of the program; a downturn in sales may wipe out the bonus pool, leaving the employees to feel unconsciously "punished," as if management had revoked their customary bonuses.

8. After a period of years, management may regard the labor ratio as out of date and in need of revision; if revision results in a decrease in the bonus rate for employees, considerable friction and apprehension may arise.

Further Reading

National Center for Productivity and Quality of Working Life, *A Plant-wide Productivity Plan in Action: Three Years of Experience with the Scanlon Plan.* Washington, D.C., May 1975.

————*Recent Initiatives in Labor-Management Cooperation.* Washington, D.C., February 1976.

National Commission on Productivity and Work Quality, *Productivity,* Fourth Annual Report. Washington, D.C., March 1975.

14

Assessment Centers

An *assessment center* is a facility used to evaluate prospective managers in a simulated work setting, in order to identify those with acceptable potential for further development and promotion into the managerial ranks. Using a variety of individual and group-dynamic problems, specialists at the assessment center first challenge the abilities of the specially selected participants and then evaluate their competence in handling the problem situations. They then report their findings to the individuals and to top management, on a confidential and individualized basis. Typically, assessment center results play a part, but not necessarily a decisive one, in choosing managerial candidates.

At a typical assessment center, a group of about ten to twelve candidates assemble from parts of an organization or from various organizations. After a short orientation and adjustment period, they begin working at various simulated managerial problems. Operating in a kind of seminar style, they solve individually oriented problems, and they take turns leading group problem-solving sessions. Individual problems can include self-assessment questionnaires, written examinations covering management practices and techniques, pencil-and-paper problems to be solved, case studies to be examined and analyzed, and "in-basket" exercises.

A typical *in-basket exercise* presents the candidate, in the context of an imaginary managerial position in an imaginary organization, with a series of matters requiring management attention. These matters usually come in the form of memoranda, notes, and letters, each of which describes a separate problem. Usually, the candidate must attend to all the matters within a limited time period, often a severely limited one. This kind of exercise focuses not only on the candidate's ability to operate under pressure, but also on his or her understanding of basic managerial functions such as decision-making, priority-setting, and delegating.

Group-dynamic exercises usually include simulated problems for the group to solve. Each candidate has an opportunity to lead a group in dealing with at least one matter. These situations focus on the candidate's social and leadership skills, such as two-person face-to-face communication, conference leading, and group process observation and facilitation.

During the entire assessment period, which can range from one day to a full week (and in some cases longer), a seminar leader and one or more assistants administrate the activities of the candidates, presenting them with the challenge exercises and materials, collecting the results, and analyzing the activities of each of them. The assessment center staff members confer frequently during the progress of the assessment cycle and choose special assessment techniques if necessary to clarify aspects of certain candidates' managerial styles.

By the time the assessment cycle is finished, the staff members have compiled a fairly detailed report on each of the candidates, along with their opinions about the skills and potential of each. The use of these findings varies from one organization to another; but the accepted practice is for at least one staff member to brief each candidate comprehensively, to go over the results and the evaluator's opinions, and to ask for any questions the candidate may have. The final evaluation may also include a self-assessment by the candidate.

A typical assessment center report on a candidate is confidential, and it deals only with opinions of the center's staff as to that person's potential for success in a managerial job. The report, besides citing specific instances and skills, usually profiles the candidate's strengths and weaknesses in terms of certain pre-established areas. The report usually makes a general recommendation with regard to promotion into management, and it may offer suggestions for the candidate's continued development. Debatable questions are, "Should the contents of the center's report be completely available to the candidate? Or should certain opinions or recommendations be privileged to management attention?" Developing trends in "freedom of information" will probably tend to resolve the issue in favor of complete disclosure.

Most proponents of the assessment center concept seem to favor the use of the assessment report in a controlled way, to ensure that it does not become a "sudden death" factor in eliminating a candidate from job opportunities in management. Since management success depends on a variety of factors, including experience and learning, many experts feel the assessment findings should play only a part in a comprehensive evaluation of the candidate's potential, along with such factors as present job performance, the expressed desire to move into management, the level of experience and maturity, and the managerial potential demonstrated in day-to-day working situations.

Example

AT&T

Probably the best known and most extensive assessment center program is the one maintained by American Telephone & Telegraph Company. The organization is highly management-oriented, and encourages employee mobility throughout the Bell System and within various regions of it. Those who desire careers in management are given opportunities for training and counseling, and can request nomination for attendance at an assessment center program.

AT&T assessment centers have pioneered many of the model techniques already described. Usually an employee receives work time off to attend an assessment program with the sponsorship of his or her supervisor. At the center the employee has an opportunity not only for self-appraisal but for performance challenges and evaluation in action by trained assessment specialists. The resulting written evaluation becomes available to the employee and to his or her local management. Relatively large numbers of employees go through the AT&T programs each year. In 1976, AT&T reported that over 19,000 employees received such evaluations. Of these, about 35 percent were seen as having management potential.

Advantages

1. The use of an assessment center promotes a prevailing organizational norm of upward mobility, and it affirms the values associated with hard work and achievement as a basis for promotion, rather than secrecy and the personal preferences of higher managers.

2. Reliability of assessment reports is quite high; AT&T reports that rarely has a highly rated candidate received a management promotion and failed to perform competently; conversely, rarely has a low-potential candidate who was promoted to management actually performed as an outstanding manager.

3. The assessment procedure is based on multiple variables; it looks at the candidate from a variety of points of view and explores a variety of skills.

4. The assessment environment, away from the routine of the employee's job, provides a fresh opportunity to respond to challenge, reminiscent of one's first man-

agement assignment; and it gives a fresh look at the employee's skills. It also removes the employee from any possible psychological effects of a negative relationship with his or her current supervisor.

5. Assessment helps a prospective manager to decide whether he or she really wants, or can handle, a career in management; this tends to prevent or minimize the "crash and burn" situations wherein a new manager turns out to be unable to cope effectively with the demands of the job, fails miserably, is removed from the position, and thereafter feels embarrassed and demoralized.

Disadvantages/Problems

1. Some managers may tend to rely too heavily on assessment results in making promotion decisions concerning subordinates; in such a situation a marginal or negative assessment score is a "kiss of death."

2. The effectiveness of the center depends very heavily on the design of the program and equally on the skills of the staff of specialists who operate it; a poorly thought-out design can create confusion and lack of credibility in the results.

3. A negative score may follow a person for a long time in his or her career, possibly overriding the effects of later learning and development which increase the person's management potential. This unfortunate effect must be countered with an effective policy of using assessment center findings.

Further Reading

FLIPPO, EDWIN, *Principles of Personnel Management*. New York: McGraw-Hill Book Company, 1976.

JAFFEE, CABOT, "Some Dangers in Assessment Centers," *Behavioral Sciences Newsletter*, November 28, 1977.

15

Management by Objectives (MBO)

Management by objectives (MBO) is an approach to management that depends on the identification of company, departmental, and individual, objectives for a given period. It relies on defining end results, identifying the opportunities for improvement, planning action to exploit these opportunities and reviewing the outcome of the action. The three essential elements of any MBO program are:

1. a definition of the starting point or present position,

2. the specification of the finishing point, and

3. a stated time by which the identified goals have to be achieved.

This system is based on the principle that since good management is essential to the achievement of results, a manager must identify what these results should be and commit himself or herself to their achievement; therefore each individual, in conjunction with his or her superior, defines the results each achieves in order that the organization can achieve its overall objectives.

MBO is not a new concept. In fact, it is really just common sense, and most competent managers apply its principle, even if they do not call it "MBO." However, many managers work towards their own departmental objectives rather than towards the overall company objectives, thus sometimes creating a disparity between the two. Also, many people never know what objectives they are trying to achieve, and this is still often so today.

The term MBO was first used by Peter Drucker in *The Practice of Management* in 1955. He made three main points in this book relating to the approach:

1. For a business to be successful, all managers' jobs must be directed towards the objectives of the business.

2. Managers should set their own objectives and be able to control their own future.

3. Management development is essentially self-development of the manager under the guidance of the boss.

Not until the mid-1960s did systems develop that could incorporate Drucker's ideas effectively. Theorists such as George Odiorne developed systems that provided for the identification of objectives at various organizational levels and for creating plans to meet them. The system of MBO developed by John Humble gained considerable popularity in the United Kingdom. Humble extended Drucker's ideas and developed them into a practical and comprehensive form that could be used by organizations there.

Methods and Procedures

Although various theorists and practitioners vary somewhat in their actual approaches to setting up MBO programs, most of them include certain common elements. The common stages in MBO shown in Figure 15-1, are as follows:

1. organizational strategic and tactical plans,

2. unit objectives and improvement plan,

3. individual managers' improvement plans, and

4. individual review and control.

1a. Organization strategic plan

1b. Tactical plans

4. Individual review and control

2. Unit objectives and improvement plan

3. Individual manager's
—key result areas
—improvement plan

Figure 15-1

1. Organizational Strategic and Tactical Plans

Top management defines the objectives of the organization and draws them up into a *strategic* plan. An outline made of the steps required to achieve the objectives is known as the *tactical* plan.

2. Unit Objectives and Improvement Plan

The overall objectives of the organization are then disseminated to the managers of particular units or departments. Overall objectives are given in the form of goals that the unit should achieve, together with an improvement plan which will help in the fulfillment of their objectives.

3. Individual Managers, Key Result Areas, and the Improvement Plan

Each manager's job is analyzed and a management guide is produced. This guide specifies the main areas of responsibility (key result areas) of the job holder, the results to be achieved, and the means by which the progress can be monitored and measured.

The job holder and his senior agree on short-term objectives for the key areas enumerated in the management guide. These objectives are to be achieved within a defined period, and a job improvement plan is produced.

4. Individual Review and Control

The manager carries out his or her job using the management guide and day-to-day talks with the boss as control information. The manager has normal contact with the boss, but at regular intervals time is set aside to meet with the boss formally in order to report on progress. Since both try to work out why objectives were not achieved, the meeting is not so much a review of the job holder as it is a review of how well the job is fulfilling its defined purpose. It mainly determines what actions need to be taken to ensure that what should be happening will happen. Difficulties are discussed, new targets agreed on, and training needs are identified for individual development. This review can help assess present performance standards as well as potential for promotion or alternative types of work.

The session usually ends with the drawing up of a fresh plan of action for the next period.

The process of control and review continues for both the individual managers and the organization as a whole. Top management reviews the progress toward objectives and at least once a year updates the long-range plan. The cycle is thus a continuous one that ensures that the organization's policy is kept up to date and that the policy is implemented as effectively as possible.

MBO can be implemented by management consultants or by a management adviser appointed and trained from within the company. These advisers assist top management in clarifying objectives and ensuring that these are understood by other managers. They assist each job holder and his senior to achieve a mutual understanding of key results, levels of performance, and the associated

control. They also help to provide ideas for improvement
and the like.

Example

Simon Engineering Dudley, Ltd.

A fully owned subsidiary of Simon Engineering, Ltd.,
Dudley employs three hundred people engaged in the
design, manufacture, and servicing of a range of devices
for fire-fighting and rescue operations.

MBO was introduced in 1968, on the recommendation of an international consulting firm engaged initially
by the holding company in a corporate planning assignment. A consultant was assigned to the job, and stage 1 of
the program began with the preparation of management
guides for all senior and middle management and carried
on according to the MBO method.

Soon after the introduction of MBO, a number of
difficulties and problems had arisen:

1. MBO was too heavily "personnel" oriented, towards
   management appraisal and development.

2. The scheme was introduced from the bottom without
   first defining and completing the overall company objectives.

3. A mistake occurred in the timing of the introduction
   of MBO as the managing director was changed four
   months after its introduction—which created further
   problems.

4. Enthusiasm for the scheme was lacking among the managers concerned.

5. The management guides and action plans in the first draft shape were not consistent with overall company objectives.

The lessons learned from these problems were that:

1. MBO must be applied as a *management style* that is dynamic, adaptable, and motivating enough for managers to achieve company objectives.

2. Defining company objectives is necessary, as well as developing MBO from board level down and not only upwards from the shop floor.

3. MBO must be implemented by means of participation and understanding, not through fear brought about by using it as a management appraisal weapon.

4. Successful application depends on the enthusiastic cooperation of all board members and managers.

Having learned these lessons, the company started again. It adopted the techniques of the Humble method of MBO but applied them to suit its own company operation and adapted them to suit its own management style. The company believed it important that MBO should be introduced in the language that the management team understood.

This time the management team participated as a whole in deciding on company objectives and a strategic plan covering five years. This plan was devised under the six headings of general strategy, profitability, marketing, innovation, production, and human resources. The six areas were then broken down into quantifiable sections where appropriate and practical in terms of measurement and control. These objectives were set down in a "Yellow Book," and every manager knew where he or she and the company were going.

The next stage was to prepare individual management guides and action plans within the framework of the company objectives. These would allow job holders to identify key result areas, define acceptable standards of performance when the job was being well done, and provide simple and accurate means of measuring performance.

Managers were prepared by ensuring that all board members and departmental heads possessed copies of the company objectives and strategic plan, together with the tactical plan. Given this picture, each individual director and manager should be capable of setting his or her own key tasks, defining standards of performance, and suggesting means of measuring results. All this was done with the aid of an MBO adviser.

Some difficulties did arise in drawing up management guides and action plans. Some were too detailed or not detailed enough, and most were too optimistic in the setting of targets. Keeping plans simple was found to be best.

The scheme is monitored by eight meetings a year of management and quarterly board meetings. Progress is monitored against the company objectives; strategic and tactical plans, action plans, and management guides are altered where necessary.

The advantages that managers feel MBO has brought to the company are:

1. It has given them a management style that suits the company, and it enables management to participate in

the running of the business to achieve the desired results.

2. It provides a framework for a dynamic and adaptable style of leadership.

3. MBO is used as a means of achieving growth and profits—it is not an end in itself. The end is not management appraisal and development; this is only a byproduct of MBO.

4. The system provides "on the job" training for all participants.

5. It has helped to improve communication.

Advantages

1. It brings out the need for the clarification of objectives at the top of an organization. This in itself has led to modifications of policy, redirection of management effort, elimination of overlapping jobs, and increase of productivity. Thus it is an effective way to encourage long-term planning instead of only short-term commitments.

2. It draws out valuable suggestions for improvement from management at every level.

3. It gives each manager a clearer picture of the most important areas of work and the results he or she is expected to achieve. It also provides standards against which to measure progress.

4. It provides an effective means of clarifying the tasks of subordinates, and helps with the delegation of authority and responsibility.

5. It helps assess the performance of staff members and identify their needs in a positive manner.

6. It may improve morale, enthusiasm, and commitment through greater participation in the organization's affairs and in the setting of one's own objectives.

7. It forces managers to think of planning for results rather than merely planning activities or work. It also helps to ensure that realistic goals are set.

8. A major strength of MBO is clarification of the ideal structure of the organization so that its objectives can be achieved.

9. A training and management development program can be introduced, related to individual and departmental objectives. This program provides better management training at a lower cost.

10. It helps with the identification of employees' potential so that reliable management succession plans can be built up.

Disadvantages/Problems

1. Some systems involve much paperwork; the major pitfall to be avoided is the natural tendency to concentrate at the outset on the system itself and the associated documentation rather than on the purpose and the concepts involved.

2. Through poor implementation, MBO might be seen as a gimmick; people may go through the motions and fill in the appropriate paperwork, but the spirit will be gone.

3. Achievable and meaningful goals are difficult to set especially as they involve the future, with all its uncertainties. The major problem is to set goals that are reasonably but not easily obtainable: These must not be too difficult to achieve nor too easy; people who are not stretching their abilities become frustrated.

4. MBO could lead to so much attention being paid to setting and achieving a few major objectives that managers will overlook other aspects of their jobs, or they may push their own objectives at the expense of the organization's.

5. One of the great weaknesses of using performance against objectives as the standard of measuring managerial action is that a manager can meet or miss goals through no fault of his or her own. The appraisal may be centered on personality rather than performance.

6. Although MBO is a simple system, it is not easy for people to learn and it is not self-teachable, because it is difficult to plan for clear end-results.

7. Maintaining an environment that makes MBO work takes effort throughout the company, and it may take as long as three years to get understanding and commitment.

8. One of the major reasons for ineffectual MBO is the failure to give the guidelines to the goal-setters. They need to understand the end-result for which they are responsible and how this result contributes to corporate objectives.

9. When goals are being set, one man's objectives may be inconsistent with those of another, so goals must be interrelated and supportive.

10. Goals must not be forced onto an individual by the boss, or else the system may not be truly participative.

11. Fuzzy objectives must be avoided and goals should be verifiable in a quantitative or qualitative way, so that at some target time in the future a manager can know whether or not he or she has reached the goals.

12. Inflexibility is a latent danger in the system. Events may require a change in goals that may not in fact take place.

13. Review and counseling of managers may not be adequate. A boss must have regular information on subordinates and not just forget about them.

14. If management development is carried out only on the basis of data from the performance appraisal, it may be unsatisfactory, as other factors should be considered.

15. The system must be appropriate to the organization; everyone's support within a given sector is required, or the system breaks down.

16. Training is required to carry out appraisals.

17. MBO may be seen by management as a means of controlling subordinates as they can no longer pass the buck. Some, too, may see it as a refined piecework system to keep increasing subordinates' output.

18. It may become too narrow and remove initiative; also, motivation may fall off after a while.

Further Reading

ALBRECHT, KARL, *Successful Management by Objectives: An Action Manual*. Englewood Cliffs, N.J.: Prentice-Hall, Inc., 1978.

HUMBLE, JOHN, *How to Manage by Objectives*. New York: Amacom, 1972.

ODIORNE, GEORGE, *Management by Objectives*. New York: Pitman, 1965.

16

Organization Development (OD)

Organization development (OD) is a process of planned change that involves behavioral science techniques designed to build a more effective organization. It concentrates on creating an open-minded, flexible organization that is receptive to change, one in which the people involved can recognize the need for change and implement any action themselves. Initially a "change agent" is usually required to help the individuals plan for change and bring it about. Unlike traditional training methods, it concentrates on the total organization, the total unit, rather than on individual development; it focuses on organizational, group, and interpersonal processes. OD can be applied profitably to an organization of any size, ranging from a ten-person working unit, up to a multi-plant company, government agency, hospital, college, military command, or any other kind of socio-technical system.

Modern organizations are faced, more than ever before, with the need for change arising from technological demands—changes in the market, changes in labor skills, and changes in the attitudes of employees. Today's employee usually wants more participation in decision-making and greater job satisfaction. Other changes can arise from mergers, new management teams, an increase in size, and the need to improve performance. Given these pressures for changes, any approach must accommodate change and the initiation of change *within* the organization.

Further, conventional training methods apparently have little long-term effect on individual or departmental performance, for a number of reasons:

1. Senior line management may view training as achieving only short-term economic objectives and have no real commitment to long-term training. Managers often become disillusioned when training courses seem to fail to provide the solutions to the problems they define.

2. The training staff may be forced into the role of only providing training courses, either because they are not allowed to become involved in problem-solving or because they lack the caliber and skills required for an OD approach.

3. People who are at the receiving end of traditional training courses often become disillusioned and frustrated, because they may not be allowed to implement

their newfound ideas once they are back in the job situation.

Although many companies recognize the need for developing effective human relations and flexible management styles, they tend to concentrate on the individual rather than on social roles operating within a certain authority structure.

Three possible approaches can be used to bring OD techniques into an organization:

1. External OD consultants can be used on a contract basis for specific change programs.

2. Internal managers can be used who are specialists using behavioral science techniques to facilitate planned changes.

3. The role of the personnel manager and/or the training specialist can be developed to incorporate an OD role.

Whichever resource is used, the aim of the consultant or change agent is to work himself or herself out of a job by improving the organization's capacity for self-help.

Features of an OD Activity

The general approach to an organization development program is sometimes referred to as the *action-research model,* which implies a cyclic process of researching the organization's social functioning, taking action to improve it, reassessing it, taking new actions, and so on. OD is ideally a continuous process, based on an enlightened approach to top management, rather than an isolated event in the organization's history. This cyclic process of planned change is analogous to the medical cycle of "diagnosis–prescription–remedy." Another typical formulation is the four-phase concept of assessment, planning, action, and follow-through.

Arcane terminology abounds in the OD field, as it does in most areas heavily oriented to the behavioral sciences. The curious term "action-research," for example, may have been coined to soften the possible negative reactions of hardbitten workaday managers to the idea of research, with its customary connotation of something done in the university setting. In any case, it is vitally important that any OD program follow a carefully planned approach of this general form.

An OD activity uses experience-based material as a means of analyzing an organization's culture. Techniques used in OD are largely group-oriented and can include such methods as attitude surveys, sensitivity training, work restructuring, appraisal, briefing groups, team-building exercises, and organizational analysis. The progression of a typical program is roughly as follows:

1. First consultations take place between the senior executives and the change agent; the general aims of the program as well as the ideas and concepts underlying it, are discussed. Further, there is a preliminary discussion of problems that are of immediate concern to the participants.

2. The diagnostic stage follows. Stock is taken of such organizational processes as climate, morale, opinion,

feelings, interpersonal relationships, and the like. Any strengths and weaknesses can be diagnosed by questionnaires, interviews, observations, and diagnostic meetings. A plan is then devised to clarify the objectives to be achieved.

3. The next step is team development. Here an attempt is made to resolve some of the problems of understanding, communication, interpersonal relationships, and conflict within the various teams involved in the process and to apply some of the lessons learned to the day-to-day problems.

4. Inter-team training then takes place where the aims are to achieve better understanding between department and functions and to improve vertical and horizontal communications.

5. The next stage is to set improvement targets and to examine potential problems and difficulties. Alternative plans of action may be considered.

6. Implementing agreed changes comes next, along with modifying the original plans in the light of experience.

7. The final stage is to monitor results and maintain the newly established methods and procedures.

The teams usually meet on a part-time basis and are given the opportunity to analyze problems and, with specialist help or advice, to study some of the human and behavioral problems involved. Members are encouraged to speak openly about their perceptions of problem areas. They may undertake team-building exercises and intergroup activities that encourage them to do this and to build on one another's strengths.

Example

TRW, Inc.

TRW, Incorporated of Redondo Beach, California, has long used an OD approach to the development of effective special project teams to carry out its highly technical and complex aerospace development programs. When the company wins a contract for a large-scale experimental or developmental project, a program manager is appointed to lead the effort. This person assembles a special project team, consisting usually of a small group of "permanent" members, as well as a larger selection of functional specialists who report formally to the managers of various specialty groups but who work directly under the guidance of the program manager. These team members are chosen primarily for their expertise in the various technical areas critical to the successful completion of the project.

Then the program manager draws on the expert assistance of the in-house organization development group, whose trained specialists help in the process of welding the new group of people—many of whom may not have worked together before—into an effective and efficient team. Using the various OD techniques, such as interviews, group training activities, team-building workshops, and occasional task-oriented feedback sessions, the OD practitioners help the individuals of the project team to develop skills and methods for dealing with one another effectively in carrying out their various assignments.

TRW also uses an OD approach to its overall management process, which sets a very constructive backdrop for this project-level team-building. Human resources development (HRD) people periodically use employee sensing techniques, such as attitude survey questionnaires and sampling interviews, to spot emerging problems or issues that might adversely affect morale or job performance. These data become part of the management information base required to guide the organization and plan its HRD programs.

Advantages

1. The OD approach brings into the open the *real* human problems of the organization and makes them known and understood by the people at the top of the hierarchy.

2. It concentrates on the teamwork approach, rather than on individual development which can lead to better morale and possibly greater efficiency, at the level of overall units or departments.

3. It is appropriate for an organization that exists in a rapidly changing environment, as it helps people face change effectively.

Disadvantages/Problems

1. The OD approach may at times cause stresses and strains with established practices and procedures. For instance, how does one reward workers who have

   doubled their production when their pay rate system
   is not directly geared to production?

2. The main disadvantage of implementing OD is that its
   potential cannot be demonstrated without the entire
   involvement of the very people one needs to influence. If they are suspicious at the outset, they are not
   going to cooperate; and OD is a technique that cannot
   be imposed.

3. OD programs must be designed to meet the particular
   purpose of the organization in which they are being
   run.

4. An OD program cannot achieve miracles overnight,
   and such a program will be costly in terms of time and
   resources.

5. A program will rarely be successful if members of top
   management do not experience external or internal
   pressure for change and if they do not take part in the
   planning of change.

Further Reading

ARGYRIS, CHRIS, *Management and Organization Development.* New
   York: McGraw-Hill Book Company, 1971.
BENNIS, WARREN, *Organization Development: Its Nature, Origins and
   Prospects.* Reading, Mass.: Addison-Wesley, 1969.

17

Equal Employment Opportunity (EEO)

An *equal employment opportunity (EEO)* program is an organization-wide effort to ensure that no worker or prospective worker is denied any opportunity related to employment, pay, or advancement, through discrimination on the basis of personal characteristics or factors that have nothing to do with competent performance of the job. Such a program usually includes organizational assessment, planning, and follow-through in a variety of forms. A specific goal of an EEO program is to have women and members of "protected" minority groups represented within the organization's structure—including at all levels of management—in roughly the same proportions as they are represented in the community from which the organization draws its labor force.

Since the early 1960s, civil rights legislation has focused strongly on economic opportunity, a major component of which is, of course, job opportunity. The Civil Rights Act of 1964 contained a provision known to personnel people as "Title VII," which identified as unlawful those employment practices that discriminated against people on the basis of racial, religious, or ethnic characteristics. Title VII identified the five key discrimination factors of race, color, religion, sex, and national origin. Subsequent legislation amended and extended this law to cover discrimination on the basis of age—for people between the ages of 45 and 65—and on the basis of physical handicaps that did not interfere with job performance. The Civil Rights Act of 1964 also created the Equal Employment Opportunity Commission and empowered it to prosecute in the district courts all cases it considered matters of discrimination. Most states established implementing mechanisms of their own, both for state and local employees and for private concerns operating in the states. A series of presidential Executive Orders instructed Federal agencies that transacted contract business with private firms to require all but the smallest firms to show evidence of "affirmative action" to establish and maintain equal employment opportunity conditions within their organizations.

Although the terms EEO and Affirmative Action are often used interchangeably, they are actually two distinct requirements. EEO refers to the general concept of preventing discrimination, while AA refers to the specific requirements for planning and programming required of firms that do substantial amounts of contract business with Federal agencies. It has become customary, however, for most organizations to have Affirmative Action plans as part of their overall EEO programs. For this reason, EEO and AA are becoming more and more closely linked.

A great deal of EEO theory and practice stems from *case law*—the recognized body of guidance resulting from specific landmark court decisions. Personnel specialists must work diligently to stay abreast of the developing legal basis of EEO, especially since the area has become a virtual playing field for attorneys. Since the purpose of this discussion is simply to present an overview of the basic concepts of EEO, it will be confined to the more straightforward features of the matter of discrimination.

For EEO purposes, any action on the part of an employer's representative—personnel specialist, supervisor, or anyone else—is said to constitute discrimination if it has two basic effects:

1. If it results in the *disparate treatment* of members of any protected group, that is if it tends to favor certain people and hinder others solely on the basis of race, color, religion, sex, age or national origin; *and*

2. If it results in *adverse impact* on the members of the group who received the disparate treatment, that is, if they stand to be deprived of opportunities for getting jobs, keeping jobs, being trained and developed for advancement, getting promoted, or being fairly paid for their work.

The basic concept of EEO is that an organization should manage the personnel function (which involves recruiting, hiring, job placement, training and development, compensation, proper supervision on the job, promotion and advancement, and termination when appropriate) without regard to arbitrary factors that cannot be shown to affect the person's performance on the job and consequently his or her value to the organization. Such job requirements as being male or female or being under twenty-five years old, for example, can rarely be shown to be necessary for adequate job performance. Consequently, ruling people out solely on this basis is usually declared discriminatory. Conversely, ruling out a person who is unable to climb about on high structures, if the job requires it, can seldom be shown to be discriminatory. The important thing in rejecting a candidate for hiring or promotion is the job requirement itself, not the presumption that all members of some category—such as handicapped people or women or Asians—cannot do the work. This unrebuttable presumption of incompetence, as attorneys call it, is an illegal employment practice.

Equal employment opportunity, or the lack of it, is usually rooted deep in the sociology of the organization itself. Widespread discrimination usually reflects top management's unawareness or tacit acceptance, together with culturally derived—often unconscious—discrimination among the key people of the organization, who more or less make the rules about how employees or applicants are treated and what opportunities are open to them. True equality of opportunity usually reflects a highly aware top management, and an enlightened form of management practice at all operating levels.

An EEO program usually starts with a comprehensive assessment of the organization's personnel practices, along the entire chain of events from recruiting to termination. A study of the composition of the work force yields a statistical summary of its make-up, in terms of men and women, blacks, latinos, and Asians, age ranges, physical handicaps, and religious affiliation if appropriate. It is important in taking such data that individuals remain anonymous with respect to their key characteristics, and that the analysis be done on a "blind" statistical basis. Personnel practice tends to exclude from employee records such data as ethnic origin, marital status, and sometimes even age, in order to reduce the likelihood of discrimination or charges of discrimination. Many companies also review certain kinds of jobs to determine whether they have become stereotyped in favor of certain kinds of people; and they review others to see whether they have been stereotyped in ways that tend to exclude certain categories of people. Special attention often goes to the number of women in management positions, since management has traditionally been a male function in American organizations.

If the analysis shows certain kinds of people underrepresented in the work force, in proportion to the general population of the surrounding community, then steps are usually necessary to improve the situation. Customarily, an Affirmative Action plan is drawn up with specific goals and timetables for achieving them. Typically, these goals become operating targets not only for personnel people, who attempt to meet them through changes in recruiting and hiring practices, but also for the managers, who attempt to meet them through careful attention to training and promotion practices.

The analysis usually includes a thorough review of all *screening devices* used by personnel people, such as recruiting advertisements, job application forms, hiring interviews, tests and other assessment instruments, placement methods, employee records, and performance evaluations. Those tools that seem to contribute to disparate treatment or adverse impact on certain kinds of individuals are eliminated or redesigned. Personnel and supervisory practices come under the same scrutiny. The guiding policy, the paramount factor in all personnel actions, is job performance. Jobs must be defined in terms of performance. If this is done adequately, then screening decisions can be made solely on the basis of a particular individual's ability to perform the work, rather than on the basis of arbitrary characteristics that assign the individual to some abstract category or other.

The result of this analysis and planning phase is typically the Affirmative Action plan, which spells out what needs to be done over a given period (such as one to five years), who is responsible for getting it done, and how performance against the goals will be measured. It is also customary for top management to issue a comprehensive policy statement, setting forth executive guidance and support for the goals of the program in particular and for equal employment opportunity in general. A staff EEO officer is also customarily appointed, although very few organizations grant the EEO officer very much authority.

Advantages

1. A formal EEO program focuses attention on the problem of discrimination and tends to make it less likely, at least overtly.

2. An EEO program not only gives top management some specific measures of its performance in the human resources area, but it also keeps attention focused on the social responsibility of the organization.

3. It provides a basis for specific, concrete actions by designated individuals within the organization who are in

a position to affect the employment opportunities of workers and prospective workers.

4. Formal programs and reporting systems enable compliance agencies to focus attention on industries and organizations where discrimination is strongest.

5. An EEO program can play a part in improving the utilization of human resources and increasing productivity, by activating the potential of talented people who might otherwise remain locked into low-performance jobs and demotivating situations.

Disadvantages/Problems

Unfortunately, the term "EEO" usually carries connotations of legal battles with government agencies and employee lawsuits in the mind of the typical executive. This is often a fact of life, as some overzealous compliance officials operate in a clumsy, heavy-handed way, creating resentment and animosity among the executives of the organizations they attack. This adversary mentality leads to a number of disappointments in making EEO programs effective. For example:

1. Many traditional-minded hard-bitten executives are confirmed in their cynicism toward women and minority group members by punitive government actions.

2. Many top management groups merely give lip service to the EEO program, hoping they won't have any serious legal problems.

3. Huge punitive cash settlements and awards for back wages made by district courts, together with the legal profession's policy of contingent fee scales, has turned the area of EEO litigation into a lucrative field for lawyers. This unfortunate byproduct of the law has severely aggravated relations between corporations and compliance agencies, and it has made personnel people extremely defensive. The "class action" lawsuit, filed against an organization on behalf of all employees supposedly discriminated against in the past, has created great hardship, expense, and ill feeling in the area of EEO compliance.

4. Irate employees sometimes file complaints of discrimination after being discharged for legitimate causes, requiring companies to spend large sums for legal services and staff time in defending the actions of their managers.

5. The huge backlog of claims accumulating in the various compliance offices means that an employee with a legitimate claim of discrimination must usually wait for as long as two to three years before his or her claim gets resolved; the original purpose—to remedy the disadvantage caused to the employee—is often lost.

6. Managers and personnel people sometimes become very defensive and overly cautious in disciplining women and minority employees who truly deserve it, for fear of triggering discrimination complaints; many organizations establish elaborate, time-consuming, and costly documentation procedures for disciplinary actions for the same reasons.

7. Like so many other government programs, the enforcement process has for the most part missed its

original objectives and has led to the expenditure of enormous sums of money by government and industry alike. It cannot be said that great progress has been made in creating truly equal opportunity within the labor marketplace. A great deal of what has been accomplished can probably be attributed to the efforts of activist groups and the effects of public attention, just as much as to the activities of government compliance agencies.

Further Reading

"Equal Employment Opportunity Act of 1972," Washington, D.C.: U.S. Government Printing Office, 1972.

MEGGINSON, LEON C., *Personnel and Human Resource Administration*. Homewood, Ill.: Richard D. Irwin, Inc., 1977.

18

Behavior Modification (Be-Mod)

Behavior modification (Be-Mod), as used in management practice, is the specification of desired "target" behaviors on the part of employees and the systematic arrangement of the work situation so as to reinforce those behaviors, making them more frequent and consistent. Although a few practitioners take a rather covert, manipulative approach to changing employee behavior, accepted practice involves a cooperative program of planned change. In most cases, managers and employees agree on the kinds of behavior change desired, such as punctual arrival at the work site, economizing on consumable materials or resources, special actions to achieve a particular quality standard, or specific selling behaviors in dealing with customers. They then analyze the process of performing the desired actions and identify specific *contingencies,* or immediate outcomes, that can be built into the situation to automatically reinforce the desired behavior.

Many managers not familiar with the behavioral sciences are appalled at first at a new concept that seems to treat the employee as if he or she were a laboratory animal, to be manipulated like a mindless robot. Some lay writers, having only a vague grasp of the actual implementation of behavior modification programs, have painted lurid pictures of a "brave new world" society in which everyone moves about mindlessly and obediently in response to a totally controlled environment.

A more enlightened view of human behavior, however, shows that whenever two human beings are interacting with each other, they are actually continuously modifying each other's behavior in a complex interchange of action and reaction. Each is trying to get certain responses from the other. The technology of behavior modification merely makes this everyday phenomenon a conscious, planned process. For example, when a manager unconsciously displays a punitive, accusative, aggressive managerial style in dealing with employees, he or she rapidly shapes their behavior into an avoidance pattern. They tend to interact with the boss less frequently and usually only after explicit direction to do so. By providing them with *negative reinforcement* for their communicative behavior, he unconsciously extinguishes it. As a result of the negative contingency that follows his or her visit to the boss's office, the employee visits the office less and less frequently.

Conversely, a manager who treats employees with

warmth and encouragement, who listens carefully and accurately, and who gives positive feedback can shape the employee's behavior in such a way as to increase the frequency of constructive visits to the office. The manager and the employee may or may not be consciously aware of this process unless they stop to think it over, in which case the cause-and-effect relationship becomes apparent—and appreciated.

Behavior modification as a management technique is based firmly on the principles of *operant conditioning,* developed in the early 1930s by Dr. B. F. Skinner at Harvard University. According to Skinnerian psychology, all behavior in the long run is a function of its consequences. That is, a person (or any other creature for that matter) tends to repeat and intensify a behavior if the immediately perceived consequences are positive, that is, if the consequences constitute something the person wants or enjoys. Desirable consequences are almost limitless, including a smile or praise from a manager, positive feedback from a co-worker, a complimentary note or memo, bonus pay if received soon and directly in response to the target behavior, or even an occasional signal from a machine or instrument telling the worker he has performed well. Conversely, a person tends to repeat a behavior less often if the direct consequences are perceived as undesirable. The more undesirable and repeatable the consequences, the more rapidly the person abandons the behavior.

The contingencies, or consequences, provided to shape the behavior are defined as *positive reinforcers* and *negative reinforcers,* according to whether they lead the person to behave in ways that intensify or diminish the outcomes, respectively. Negative reinforcers seem to abound in the business organization, including scolding or critical remarks made by the manager, hostility from one's co-workers, feelings of frustration at being unable to complete a task, antagonistic behavior by customers or clients, and lost pay or loss of an expected bonus or commission.

This simple theory does not require any notion of the inner needs, feelings, and thoughts of the employee to get results. It merely requires that the manager first specify very clearly and objectively one or more employee behaviors to be reinforced, and then specify the behaviors to be reduced or eliminated. If he or she can provide contingencies in the employee's environment that increase or decrease the target behaviors, the employee automatically finds the new behaviors comfortable, successful, and likeable.

Although this principle of behavior modification is simple and readily acceptable on a logical basis, many managers behave as if they do not understand it or do not believe it. Making the principle work often takes a good deal of careful thought. Punishment is much more a fact of life in our culture than reward. For example, if a shop foreman stands next to the time clock and glares at employees who clock in late, without reinforcing those who arrive early, he may only succeed in teaching the latecomers to invent better and more imaginative excuses for being late. Coercion and critical remarks can reduce the lateness to some extent. But actually, the employees probably experience the situation as *being caught* rather than being late. If the foreman can't stand there every day or if there are several clock-in stations, the desired behavior of arriving on time may not increase. In this case the undesired behavior has been punished in a haphazard way, but the desired behavior has not been rewarded.

Similarly, managers often scold and criticize employees, hoping to get them to work more effectively.

Criticism seldom has a very strong effect in reinforcing desired behavior, although it can work to reduce undesired behavior. Criticism usually makes an employee feel defensive but not necessarily committed to the new behavior the manager desires. A more effective managerial approach is to recognize the new behavior when the employee exhibits it, or even a small sample of it, and to give praise or other positive reinforcers immediately. If on-time arrival is truly important, a *contingency system* can be set up in which a point is scored for each timely arrival. Though the points themselves can function as reinforcers of a kind, if the employees can earn a small bonus for a number of consecutive on-time arrivals, then they will experience the results of punctuality as positive and desirable.

In the light of how extremely simple this concept is, it is truly remarkable how many managers steadfastly adhere to essentially punitive social tactics, when the much more effective procedure is to detect and reward the desired behavior and to simply ignore the undesired behavior. Punitive behavior on the part of the manager only leads to defensiveness on the part of the employees and usually a search for avoidance strategies. Rewarding desired behavior, on the other hand, is attractive rather than repulsive; it is simply a matter of presenting a properly selected consequence as a result of the behavior to be reinforced.

A very simple application of the behavior modification concept is to make a survey of working conditions, job tasks, and daily activities from the point of view of the employees in a work unit. By identifying and removing the consequences that tend to reduce or eliminate desired behavior and by adding positive reinforcers, the manager can usually improve work performance and can often improve morale at the same time.

A typical application of programmed behavior modification involves the following steps:

1. specifying the desired behaviors to be developed; these should be simple, few in number, and directly connected to measurable results that have recognized value in terms of organizational performance;

2. measuring the current level of the desired behavior to establish a baseline;

3. choosing target levels of the behavior to be achieved;

4. designing a contingency system, that is, a controllable set of outcomes that can be matched with the desired behaviors, usually in cooperation with the employees who are to achieve the new behavior levels;

5. implementing the contingency system and measuring changes in the behavior levels, also in cooperation with the employees;

6. revising and tuning up the contingency system as necessary; and

7. confirming the new behavior levels and making them permanent by establishing contingencies that continue to reinforce the target behavior.

In some cases, the change agents involved may temporarily remove the contingencies for a short period, to see whether the behaviors tend to return to their former levels. If so, they reapply the contingencies and if the behaviors achieve the target levels again, they take this renewed behavior to mean that the chosen contingencies are indeed effective reinforcers.

Examples

Ingalls Shipbuilding Division

Litton Industries applied behavior modification techniques in its Ingalls Shipbuilding Division, with the simple aim of preventing injuries by getting workers to wear safety glasses and gloves. One group of supervisors was trained to observe workers for the target behavior and to positively reinforce it with verbal recognition, encouragement, and occasional compliments. A control group of supervisors was trained to merely observe the behavior. After a short period, the test-group employees had increased their safety behavior markedly, and the control group showed no corresponding improvement.

Cost Savings at Emery Air Freight

Another prominent area for application of this emerging technique is in cost savings. A number of firms have targeted on employee behaviors that can reduce costs by cutting down on process time, by reducing waste, by improving scheduling of interactive tasks, by upgrading preventive maintenance of machinery, and by reducing errors in recordkeeping. Proponents of behavior modification contend that virtually any organization can achieve very significant improvements in operating economy by the fairly straightforward application of readily available techniques.

One of the most widely studied programs, at Emery Air Freight, resulted in a considerable documented cost saving. Unusually high error rates in filling orders and packing them into shipping containers led to a program of contingency management that provided reinforcers for accurate and effective work. By analyzing the chains of behavior involved in the work process, managers were able to spot key disincentives to accurate performance and to supply the missing incentives. Most of these added incentives for accuracy were no-cost items, consisting of changes in work processes and personal reinforcement techniques learned by the supervisors. Once the supervisors learned to reinforce the desired behaviors effectively—and not necessarily every time they occurred—the new behaviors became reliable and stable. Emery Air Freight reported an estimated cost saving of about $2,000,000 as a result of the program.

A variety of other successful applications has sparked a strong interest in behavior modification. A manufacturing company reported a saving of $550,000, which amounted to a 1,900 percent return on its investment in the cost of the program. Several airlines also successfully applied the technique, to increase reservation bookings. An amusement park in California achieved outstanding levels of employee competence in customer service by arranging for customers as well as for supervisors to reinforce helpful actions.

Advantages

1. The approach is specific, performance-oriented, focused on measurable results, and readily evaluated.

2. It involves known, tested, and accepted principles of human behavior.

3. It is conceptually easy to understand.

4. It is comparatively straightforward in implementation.

5. It is adaptive, that is, management can try a variety of contingencies to ensure that the target behavior is properly reinforced.

6. Managers can learn to apply the technique to a variety of situations, after a learning period with an expert consultant or trained change agent.

7. Behavior modification programs can win the support of top management more readily than can a number of other behavioral techniques, because they can focus on measurable economic results.

Disadvantages/Problems

1. The concept has such a strong, unavoidable psychological connotation that many managers are wary of it, especially those who have had little or no training in the behavioral sciences.

2. Even people with behavioral sciences training may initially regard the technique as somehow cold-bloodedly manipulative.

3. Many managers will probably be tempted to apply the technique in a covert, secretive way, probably causing

feelings of apprehension, mistrust, and hostility among employees who feel like unwilling guinea pigs.

Further Reading

FEENEY, E. J., "Behavior Modification in Perspective," Special Report, *Behavioral Sciences Newsletter,* 1977.

GOODALL, KENNETH, "Shapers at Work," *Psychology Today* (November 1972), p. 53.

HALL, ELIZABETH, "Will Success Spoil B. F. Skinner?" *Psychology Today* (November 1972), p. 65.

MAGER, ROBERT, and PETER PIPE, *Analyzing Performance Problems, or "You Really Oughta Wanna."* Belmont, Calif.: Fearon Publishers, 1971.

Section Three

EXPERIMENTAL TECHNIQUES

This section is concerned with techniques that, while somewhat controversial and not fully proven, do nevertheless merit study for possible application in America. Most of them have originated in England or other European countries and have had limited success so far. The extent of their feasibility within the American business setting is open to discussion and is therefore necessarily left to the reader's own judgments.

19

Human Resource
Accounting*
(HRA)

Human Resource Accounting (HRA) is the system for recording measurement, in monetary terms, of the productive capability of the total human organization of a business or any other entity. Like any accounting system, it has books of account for routine expenses incurred, to be written off against current profits, and for those special expenses incurred in investment, only a part of which will be written off against current profits. Unlike conventional accounting, it is concerned with the present and future valuation of employee groups to their employing authority. Thus in

*By J. J. Hayward, Principal Lecturer, Financial Management, Kingston Polytechnic, England.

content, any HRA system may well be a comprehensive set of accounts recording the time and costs involved in reaching such decisions as employee recruitment, selection, induction, familiarization, training, job transfers, and performance appraisals. These accounts are used to help establish the values of employees' productive capability. When considering values, we are concerned with measurement and more with relative rather than absolute values. Accordingly, greater significance is usually attached to changes in the original absolute value than to its original accuracy.

The objective of HRA systems is to create and to maintain a reliable evaluation tool by which management can assess the effectiveness of change in its management of human resources. The human resource element may be all or only a part of the total employees engaged in the total entity or department. Change in their management is normally seen in the context of organization development and employee behavior.

Essentially, HRA systems are concerned with enabling management to measure the interrelationship between employees' productivity and their behavioral variables of attitude, motivation, and leadership response. HRA provides management with guidance in quantitative terms: Are funds better spent in new work restructuring or in simplifying tasks? Or on automation, less recruitment, and more training? Is management style "X" of greater mutual benefit to employer and employee than management style "Y"? And, if so, by how much and for how long?

If such a consistent reliable interrelationship could be established and measured, management of human resources should become more effective, to the mutual benefit of employer and employee. Under Renis Likert, the Institute for Social Research at the University of Michigan is attempting such measurement and has conceived HRA systems for this end. Up to the present, no positive research results have been validated from Michigan or elsewhere, and HRA systems have not developed as originally conceived but, in trying to provide some quantitative guidance to management, they have followed a "cost analysis" approach of conventional accounting.

At present all HRA systems use a cost analysis approach to the measurement of human resource productive capability or value. Consequently, they play less of a role in management guidance for more effective employment of human resources than originally conceived. These systems pay little or no heed to any interrelationship between human behavior variables as a part of organizational development and human productivity, however measured. Instead, the systems use the conventional tools, techniques, and methods of the accountant in the collection and treatment of costs for employee recruitment, selection, familiarization, and training. Collection of costs is by estimation to begin with, followed by recorded historical costs; as a result, only expenses already incurred for past events are recorded. This kind of cost treatment is like that for the physical plant and machinery of manufacturing industries—the special historical cost of buying, transporting, and installing the machine is recorded as a fixed asset able to provide long-term benefits to the business, whereas the routine maintenance and repair costs are treated as current expenses incapable of generating long-term benefits and are thus written off against current income or profits. In the same way, depreciation amounts are written off in recognition of the fact that the machine becomes less valuable—provides less future benefits—as its useful life expires.

At any one time we have depreciated asset values for

plant and machinery and also depreciated asset values for employees. This similarity of treatment has led to the term "human asset accounting." If the expected tenure of an employee is say, ten years but because of a dispute he or she resigns after only three years' service, clearly the employer has suffered a premature "loss," the reasons for which should be fully investigated. In a nutshell, the above fixed asset method shows the basic cost analysis HRA approach of expressing the amounts invested in employees, the future expected benefit periods, and their depreciated investment value at any moment. All this is based on the historical cost approach in determining original absolute values. (Subsequent change in such values still relies on historical costs but as adjusted for three key variables, as will be explained later.)

Certainly a better approach to valuation would be to measure all future potential employee group and subgroup contributions after the costs of employee acquisition, development, and management have been deducted. One could even discount these contribution benefits and related costs to present values, updating the estimated cash flows annually. But future uncertain contributions and related uncertain development costs are difficult to predict; measurement of this present value will thus always tend to be indeterminate. This difficulty is a major reason why accountants have chosen to base their valuations of fixed assets on the certain data of historical costs minus subjective values of depreciation.

In HRA systems the basic cost analysis approach of conventional fixed asset accounting is modified by upward or downward adjustment in values based on changes in three key variables:

1. replacement costs of personnel,

2. expected tenures of employees, and

3. performance potential of employees.

1. Replacement Cost Variable

This variable represents the cost of having to replace an individual at a particular moment and should probably be a closer approximation to the real investment value of an employee when compared with historical costs. Replacement values are considered particularly useful in long-range manpower planning. Of themselves, however, they cannot purport to be accurate measures of an employee's value to an employer, which is essentially a function of the other two interrelated variables of expected tenure and of performance potential over such tenure.

2. Expected Tenure Variable

This variable is analogous to the economic life of physical assets whose acquisition costs are depreciated at a rate consistent with their annual benefits to future financial periods. Human investment assets will have depreciated book values for balance sheet purposes, and, other things being equal, the employee with a longer expected tenure should have a greater book value than one with a shorter expected tenure. But unlike most fixed assets, people have considerable freedom to vary their length of service and may well appreciate in value over time. Accordingly, historical book values are periodically adjusted by changes in the factors that affect length of service: health, promotion prospects, job satisfaction, age and external opportunities.

There are obvious problems in establishing human behavioral relationships between these variables and their
impact on expected tenure. For instance, the impact of
present job satisfaction is not necessarily related to promotion prospects or age, but promotion prospects may have a
relationship with age. Nor does a long expected tenure
necessarily denote an increased "book value" since this
valuation is correct, if and only if, the actual recruitment,
selection, and development process has been done strictly
according to a well conceived and omniscient plan. The
book value acquisition cost is adjusted by the expected
tenure formula thus:

$$\frac{\text{Expected remaining tenure}}{\text{Present tenure} + \text{expected remaining tenure}} \times \begin{array}{c}\text{Current} \\ \text{replacement} \\ \text{costs}\end{array}$$

In this adjustment, changes in rather than the accuracy of, the original absolute book values are considered
important.

3. Performance Potential Variable

This variable is exceedingly difficult if not impossible
to measure. Periodic performance appraisals can help to
assess an individual's own job achievements—but where
are the measures of such an individual's potential in the
group situation: In a decision-making mode or in a risk-
taking mode?

Earlier it was suggested that an employee's value to
any employer was a function of the expected tenure and

the performance potential variables and that both were difficult to measure. Here, as in other crucial areas of HRA systems, the results of organization development experiments in measuring behavioral and productivity interrelationships are awaited. Meanwhile HRA systems following the cost analysis approach, with all their imperfections, may have to suffice as a quantitative guide to the management of human resources.

The Need for HRA Systems

The need has long been implicitly recognized, but its explicit formulation is of a much more recent origin. In the classical economists' notion of the human resource—labor—there was a complete indifference to employee expectations. The concept of profit maximization and optimum use of the factors of production, land capital, and labor treated the working population precisely as money items or as areas of land. Accordingly, workers' contributions to a firm's profits would be maximized when they were hired just up to the point where their additional income contributions equalled the additional cost for the last worker taken on. One more or less worker employed would lead to sub-optimal profits, a theory that assumed complete freedom of hire and fire, treating employees as mere agents of production.

Explicit recognition of behavioral and productivity interrelationships has, however, been granted in recent time. The need for HRA systems to measure results in economic terms of such experiments in organization development as the Hawthorne experiments (1924–27) is clear; yet interest in HRA systems has come not from students of human behavior or of OD but from the accounting fraternity. In 1962 an American accountant, Paton, argued that well organized loyal personnel could be a more important asset than stock in trade. In 1964 Hermanson wrote the monograph *Accounting for Human Assets,* at the same time as the American Accounting Association began its two-year study of accounting theory which reported the need for measurement of the interrelationship between human behavioral and financial (productivity) variables. Given this background, it is not surprising that the balance sheet asset-valuation approach has been developed, reinforced by the attempt to gauge an order of magnitude of human resource value, by equating it with those sums paid for acquisitions and mergers in excess of the recorded value of business assets. Traditionally such excess is called "goodwill," but it could be argued that this excess represents the market value, on a going concern basis, of the business asset called "human organization."

Whatever the initial impetus for accountants' interest in HRA systems, there has been and is a growing concern that conventional financial planning and control systems do de-motivate or wrongly motivate managers, an effect that, of course, works against the desired objective of improving the stability or growth of the corporate whole. Sharp disparity between punishment and reward in the financial control mechanism has taken place. For example, a divisional manager, with long-term profitability/stability in mind, is fired for not "saving costs" by his arbitrary firing of staff, cutting budgets, and so forth; at the same time, another divisional manager is promoted because he is able to report better short-term profits by the use of such "cost saving" methods. The latter kind of manager can always move on before his firm moves down. One of the major benefits of HRA systems is the proper reporting of profits made by proper management of all resources, including the human resource.

Example

R. G. Barry Corporation

All applications have been of the cost analysis type. The most widely publicized case and also the first application is that of the R. G. Barry Corporation of Columbus, Ohio. The firm employs about seventeen hundred people, with four production units, and several plants, warehouses, and sales offices located across the country. Sales expanded five-fold to $25 million from 1962 to 1969. The company makes a wide variety of leisure wear items, slippers, sandals, robes, pillows, and similar items. Typically in this type of industry, investment in fixed assets like plant, machinery, buildings, and vehicles is low; but reliance on labor-intensive processes of skilled and semi-skilled workers is high. Competitive entry into the industry thus depends vitally on being able to attract and maintain a competent, loyal labor force, which conventional accounts do not recognize.

Hence late in 1966 the firm and the Institute for Social Research, Michigan, established an HRA system experiment, including an attempt to define and measure behavioral and productivity interrelationships. By 1969 the experiment had been extended from the firm's management levels to include factory and clerical employees at two plants. Also the first HRA data ever to be published on annual reports and accounts had been accomplished in the 1969 R. G. Barry Corporation's *Report*.

A capital budget for human resources was introduced late in 1969, and managers received quarterly budget reports of the investment in human resources under their management control. These budgets inform managers whether actual development investments, or disinvestments due to employee turnover, are proceeding as planned. Conventional accounting profit figures are adjusted by amounts representing additions or reductions in the value of human resources for each profit center of the firm.

The American Accounting Association and Institute of Certified Public Accountants have both recommended that costs of recruitment and training be treated as fixed human resource assets and that they should be appropriately depreciated against future earnings benefiting from such investments in human resources. There have also been attempts to measure human resource values by assessment of such values in different positions in a firm, together with the probability of employees' ever reaching the defined positions.

HRA systems have met with some, rather limited measure of success. Both in the U.K. and France, legislation to assist industrial training could have accelerated experiments in HRA system applications, but the thrust of HRA development has stemmed not from the U.K. or France but from America, a country that still does not have industrial training legislation.

Advantages

1. Better supply, in quantitative terms, of information to management for more effective management of

human resources in total and for individual sections of the total entity.

2. Evaluation of losses from premature employee turnover.

3. Costs of planned or routine employee turnover.

4. Costs of promotion, training, and development of employees compared with their immediate or future replacement.

5. Costs of using more or less automation compared with people.

6. Computation of the extent to which short-term profit improvements are realized at the expense of liquidating human resource investments, against long-term corporate profitability and survival (the get-rich-quick-but-not-for-long syndrome).

Disadvantages/Problems

1. No sophisticated measures or computer models are needed, but extra records and initial estimates are required, using the time of managers and outside consultants, to establish original absolute values.

2. Piecemeal or phased application starting with management levels is best, to avoid increasing costs and initial mistakes of application. Time and costs of participants from management may well prove the most expensive part of system application and thus defer application.

3. "Typical" or standard costs data should be established over broad occupational groups for such items as the selection, recruitment, induction, training, and development for standard employee categories. Sampling estimation and subsequent new records will be required for this exercise as part of installation costs.

4. Periodic performance appraisals allied to the MBO approach and isolation of those factors affecting expected tenure will have to be carried out and reviewed on a regular basis.

Further Reading

GILES, W. J., and D. F. ROBINSON, *Human Asset Accounting*. IPM & ICMA, 1972.

LIKERT, RENSIS, "Measuring Organization Performance," *Harvard Business Review* (March–April 1958).

———, *The Human Organization—Its Management and Value*. New York: McGraw-Hill Book Company, 1967.

20

Employee Directors

This concept of participation refers only to the British Steel Corporation situation, as it is only in this organization, and in the John Lewis Partnership, that the United Kingdom has any experience.

Examples

British Steel Corporation

The Iron and Steel Act of 1967, which nationalized the fourteen major steel producers into the British Steel Corporation, included reference to the need for consulta-

tion and the provision of necessary information to workers' representatives to enable them to participate effectively in discussions. There was, however, no statutory requirement for the employee director scheme subsequently
set up by the Corporation.

Traditionally, participation in the steel industry had
evolved in the form of joint consultation and collective
bargaining, and there was little involvement by employees
in policy-making and at high-level decision-making. The
Employee Director Scheme was intended to allow
employees, through their representatives, to play some
part in reaching decisions that affect them. Agreement was
reached between the Corporation and the Trades Union
Congress (TUC) steel industry consultative committee on
the employee director scheme, the advantages of which
were seen to be as follows:

1. The views of shop floor employees would in this way
   be heard in the highest management committees
   operating within the Corporation's product divisional
   structure.

2. The involvement of employee directors in divisional
   management committees and in other committees
   would result in dissemination down to shop floor level
   of problems being faced and the reasons behind the
   decisions being reached.

The original proposals for the scheme included the
appointment to the boards of the various groups which—
at that time—constituted the Corporation. The appointments were made by the chairman of the Corporation
from a list presented by the steel industry consultative
committee; although employee directors were still to carry
on their old jobs, they were initially required to relinquish

any trade union offices held. Training for the role was provided on a joint basis, with courses run both by the Corporation and the TUC.

The initial scheme was reviewed by the Corporation and the steel committee in 1972. Employee directors said they felt "out on a limb" because they identified insufficiently with the other directors, with the TUC, and with fellow employees, many of whom felt suspicious of their role. By this time the Corporation itself had undergone a degree of reorganization, and the existing employee directors were serving on the boards of the six product divisions into which the Corporation had been divided. From the trade union point of view the scheme, as it stood, was inadequate for three reasons:

1. The work of employee directors was not seen as sufficiently representative of shop floor and union views.

2. The requirement to relinquish trade union offices led to a lack of contact with union machinery.

3. Although employee directors were serving on boards advisory to the divisional managing directors, executive decisions were often taken elsewhere.

Following consultation between the Corporation and the steel industry consultative committee, the scheme was modified in March 1972 by making the following changes:

1. The selection procedure was altered to allow for the greater involvement of trade union members and of the Steel Industry Consultative Committee. The final list was to be drawn up by a joint BSC/TU selection committee, and the chairman of the Corporation was to make appointments after receiving the advice and

the recommendations of this committee. Individual unions would decide for themselves the method by which local membership would be involved in making nominations.

2. Employee directors were to be allowed to continue to hold union office, and closer contact than before would be permitted with the steel industry consultative committee and national full-time officials.

3. Employee directors were to take a more active part in the consultative meetings.

4. Employee directors, while retaining an interest in all matters within their product divisions, would concentrate on those works within a "designated area" to which they were appointed and would have a close working relationship with employees in those areas.

It is probably too early to assess properly the impact of these changes. However, the employee director scheme has ceased to be regarded as experimental, and the role of employee directors has been considerably clarified.

21

Supervisory
(or Two-Tier) Boards
With Special Reference to Germany

While British company law provides for the board of directors as the only company organ besides the general meeting of shareholders, German law provides for two main organs:

1. The supervisory board, whose main function is appointing, controlling, and even dismissing the board of management.

2. The board of management, which is internally responsible for the management of the company.

"Co-determination," or worker participation, applies to the supervisory board, and in Germany there are two different systems:

The *first* system of co-determination is provided for in the 1952 Iron and Steel Act. In the iron and steel companies and coal mines, a supervisory board is composed of an equal number of workers' and shareholders' representatives, plus one independent person. In these industries the workers' representatives are appointed directly either by the competent trade union or by the works council in consultation with the trade union, and not by general election among the workers.

This co-determination law also provides for an employee director as a member of the board of management who cannot be dismissed against the majority of the worker members on the supervisory board.

There is also a general system applicable to all joint stock companies with the exception. of those in the coal, iron, and steel industries. This general system provides for the election of one-third of the members of the supervisory board by the workers of the companies and the election of the remaining two-thirds by the general assembly of the shareholders.

This system has made it possible for elected workers' representatives to participate in the most important functions of the supervisory board. Leading members of the works councils are usually those who are elected to the supervisory board, and these people know the particular conditions of the company well. There is provision for outside trade union officials to be elected, but this occurrence is rare. While this system of co-determination preserves the majority of the owners' representatives on the supervisory board, experience has shown that the workers' representatives can and do take an active interest and enjoy equal rights with the representatives of shareholders.

Advantages

1. Conflicts of interest can be contained within the supervisory board and not prejudice the effective functioning of the management board.
2. Other interests—for example the public interest, possibly local or municipal—can more easily be represented.
3. In cases of sharp conflict, the task of reconciling the needs of the company as an entity, its shareholders and employees, and the public interest could be pursued relatively free from management pressures.
4. Employee representatives do not become involved in specialized and technical discussions, where their lack of background and experience could prove a serious handicap.

Disadvantages/Problems

The drawbacks of the two-tier system parallel in many ways the advantages of the unitary board system:

1. Power and responsibility can become significantly separated. If the company got into difficulties, the

supervisory board could blame the management board for poor implementation, and the management board could blame the supervisory board for wrong instructions.

2. Important decisions requiring supervisory board approval could be harmfully delayed.

Britain

At the time of writing, the Trades Union Congress is calling on the Government to introduce a new Companies Act and new statutes for public undertakings implementing the idea of a trade union worker director. A report put out by the Labour Party says: "Our objective is the democratization of enterprises in the private sector by way of recognition of the interests of employees and increased participation by employees in the power of decision making in the company." A two-tier board structure is proposed with trade union or nominated representatives making up 50 percent of a top supervisory board and 50 percent shareholder-elected directors, plus an independent chairman.

The duties of the worker director would have to be laid out so that his responsibility would be to look after the interests of workers. Day-to-day managerial functions would be carried out by a lower board appointed by the top board, and no one should belong to both bodies. The managers would carry out policies laid out by the supervisory board on matters such as expansion or contraction of businesses and issues of mergers.

The Confederation of British Industry has warned the Government that industry will fight legislation which will give workers seats on the company boards. The CBI is opposed to a mandatory two-tier company board structure and any system that interferes with collective bargaining practices. Instead it proposes that companies should be left to experiment with worker participation proposals and to find the system best suited to their needs in terms of improving industrial relations and efficiency.

Further Reading

BROWN, I. GORDON, *Works Councils, Employee Directors, Supervisory Boards*. Institute of Public Administration, Study Paper 2.

22

Common Ownership

Common ownership is more than putting workers on company boards or giving them shares in the company. It stands for community control. To this end *the enterprise is run in the interests of the people working within it,* and not primarily for the profits of the shareholders.

Example

Scott-Bader

Scott-Bader is a British company that manufactures synthetic polymers and resins. At present it employs nearly four hundred people. In 1951 Ernest Bader, the founder and majority owner, gave his shares to an organization called the Scott-Bader Commonwealth, Ltd., and all who worked in the company could join this Commonwealth, which is legally the holding company. Until 1963, Ernest Bader and other family founder members retained the right to veto director appointments and changes in the constitution, and so they were able to guide the growth of the community at large.

Between 1951 and 1969 the following changes were introduced. The distinction between staff and manual worker status was abolished. There was no clocking in, and the same sick pay, pension schemes, and holidays applied to everyone. By 1969 much had been achieved, but the community felt it could achieve more in terms of industrial democracy. After two years of discussion, a new constitution emerged in 1971.

It was decided to simplify the organization, and it was agreed that the most valuable way to participate was by the delegation of authority and the use of representatives.

At the top of the organization is the Commonwealth, the community that holds all the shares communally. It has a board of management whose tasks are to accept Scott-Bader Company employees into membership of the Commonwealth, to distribute money to charities, and to oversee the philosophical development of the Company and the Commonwealth, that is, the total organization.

The actual running of the company is carried out by the Scott-Bader Company board. This board of directors consists of the chairman, six full-time executive members, two nonexecutive directors from outside the firm, and two members elected by the community council.

The community council, with sixteen members

elected from among all members of the Commonwealth group in constituencies of approximately twenty-five strong, is the method by which the Commonwealth members participate in the actual running of the company. Despite the fact that management, other than members of the board, are eligible to sit on the council, the members consist mainly of shop-floor people, technicians, and junior management.

The community council has wide powers. It can discuss any matter referred to it by an individual or organ of the company and can make recommendations to the board. It has the power to approve the appointment or removal of the chairman of the board and individual directors. It can itself elect two directors to the board. Further, it has the power to approve directors' remuneration, and it is the final appeal body in disciplinary disputes. Above all, it is the standing committee of members dealing with management accountability to worker-owners, that is, to all Commonwealth members.

Finally, trustees arbitrate any divergence of fundamental policy between the community council and the board.

The company also has a profit-sharing scheme that plows back a minimum 60 percent of the profits into the company. A 20 percent maximum goes as a profit share on equal basis to everyone, and a 20 percent maximum is used for charitable purposes and promoting other companies with similar aims.

Not all employees are members of the Commonwealth. The rule provides for a probationary period of six months on joining the company and then a further year on the payroll before being allowed into the Commonwealth. Only thirty people have deliberately chosen not to join.

Advantages

1. There is a high measure of security and a guarantee of no layoffs.

2. The company is free from takeovers.

3. The company is in the top one hundred of the chemical industries. Total profits have quadrupled over the last ten years.

4. There is lack of industrial unrest, with full support and cooperation from the one hundred or so union members; and there are plenty of outlets for grievances to be aired and remedied within the Commonwealth structure.

5. Labor turnover is low—7.5 percent compared with the industry's average of 18 percent.

6. It does appear to increase loyalty to the company.

Disadvantages/Problems

1. Middle management sometimes feels threatened by the extent of the participation.

2. Geographical remoteness of the company's site may explain the low turnover figures.

3. Since the company is only responsible to people working within it, it may be more insular in outlook than a company with external shareholders.

4. While this system of democracy works well at Scott-Bader, it is open to debate as to whether it would work in larger companies. This scheme may only work well in companies employing small numbers of people: If more were involved in the democratic procedures, it would eventually become too bureaucratic and slow.

Mondragón

Another interesting example of a common ownership approach to business is the network of industrial co-operatives located in the Spanish Basque community of Mondragón. Some eighty-two individual enterprises employ, and are owned by, about fourteen thousand workers. Established in 1956 by a Basque priest and several of his former students, the system expanded rapidly and diversified into a variety of industries. These include some fifty-eight manufacturing firms, a co-operative bank with seventy branches, eight housing co-ops, a regional consumer co-op, and nine educational and service co-ops. Total sales for the system amounted to $336 million in 1976, a seven-fold growth in ten years.

The guiding principles of the co-operative reflect a strong orientation toward industrial democracy. For example, the limit on the range of salaries in any one firm is three to one between the highest and lowest salaries; in other words, the highest-paid employee in the company does not earn more than three times what the lowest-paid earns. This limit is a remarkable contrast to the typical ranges of ten to one or fifteen to one in many other firms. In Mondragón co-ops, low-ranking workers earn considerably more than they would in other firms, while executives earn much less than they would elsewhere. Nevertheless, highly qualified executives and managers have tended to stay with the system, presumably because they value a sense of achievement above the monetary advantage to be gained in other companies.

Profits in each of the co-op companies are divided according to a formula. Usually 10 to 15 percent goes to the social needs of the community of Mondragón, especially for education. Another 15 to 20 percent goes into a reserve fund for the special purposes of the co-operative itself. The balance of the profit—some 65 to 75 percent— goes into a special retirement fund for the workers, held and managed by the company. Workers receive interest payments on their balances. An employee who leaves the firm may withdraw 80 percent of the balance in his or her account, and the remainder is retained by the firm. An employee who retires receives the entire amount of his or her fund balance, in addition to a pension.

The co-operative's banking system manages the retirement fund, using it for investment purposes, such as helping to establish or expand other firms within the systerm. In many ways, the Mondragón co-operative functions like a miniature, closed economic system, with highly efficient management and growth handled on a small scale.

Further Reading

"Spanish Industrial Cooperatives Achieve a Remarkable Success," *World of Work Report.* Scarsdale, N.Y.: Work in America Institute, November 1977.

Index